Mentally Challenged

Why Name Call?

Cori Coleman

authorHOUSE®

AuthorHouse™ LLC
1663 Liberty Drive
Bloomington, IN 47403
www.authorhouse.com
Phone: 1-800-839-8640

Published by AuthorHouse 11/09/2013

ISBN: 978-1-4520-0675-8 (e)
ISBN: 978-1-4520-0673-4 (sc)
ISBN: 978-1-4520-0674-1 (hc)

Library of Congress Control Number: 2010904933

This book is printed on acid-free paper.

MENTALLY CHALLENGED
BY: CORI COLEMAN

Contents

The Introduction

Our days are united with multiple situations, and these situations are making a strong impact on our daily living routines. Today, there is more than weight to bear upon our shoulders, absolute tolerance is bringing its straps over our collarbones, and it is now making its way onto our backs. And, we will continue to view our lives through a routine of self-sought differences – which we are bound to living like clockwork.

With the economy as it stands, change is in desperate need to our America.
It may seem as if we have become not only followers of a routine struggle but for some, leaders leading the followers into a burden of struggle. It is well apparent, many occupations are organized living programs; these programs are apart of a bigger orthodox plan. Every day you get up for work, the labor, the travel to the labor, and the effects – negative or positive – of the labor can be identified as a program.
Basic survival rules are if you work you will get paid, with the pay, you can purchase a lifestyle you are capable of living. Your choice will always be a selection from many of the (available) programs. Yes, programs, and I can already see the turning of your faces. Bills are one of the key factors in each program, because bills are alternate and various locations for your money. Think about it, is there anyone who receives income and are capable of placing their entire check into their bank account, and also without any destinations for their acquired earnings. And, that individual is also a middle class worker.

I did not assume so.

Much of your hard earned and slaved for income hardly belongs to you, your money has a programmed location such as housing, transportation, food, clothing, electricity, and personal responsibilities. Various occupations all over the United States are all identified by the differentiating values in annual income. Every occupation is an operation, a designed program for your chosen lifestyle. Depending on what labor you have selected, specific options have been giving to offer a system of survival. For each taxed labor in America, even a specific type of housing is assigned. If you do not believe so, get your calculator and using addition and multiplication, add and multiple what you earn to summarize exactly what you can afford. The same understanding will apply to transportation, and how it financially supports the idea of a designed program.

Potentially, the human desire for needs is just an extension of what many humans want. I remember a time where we fought for our freedom, and it appears today the more freedom we receive in one area of life, we are limited in another. Evermore is it sad the limitations that are organized for us, gaining freedom to lose only more freedom in a more complex structure of survival.

Struggle – seventy percent lower class and thirty percent middle class workers - define this scary S word. The word itself even sounds scary and it is most definitely used in a more dreadful tone of voice than favorable. You may doubt it, and more than likely due to the actions of people, but struggle is programmed into our lives as well. Debates can rage over the idea that people have a choice over their bills and over their universal struggle to live. I'd say that is about fifty percent correct. People incontrovertibly have control over their struggle, however their bills – by will – are less than controllable.

Many of us purchase our own bills, and from how it works, it will appear we have a choice or an option in that process. Any attainable bill is in someway mandatory to your selected program. Thus, you are not receiving bills by choice but in fact, you are just deciding what bill you inevitably are going to have. Buying a townhome, they – the creators of programs – can pre-determine the max amount of energy you will use in that home, in fact even in your entire neighborhood. Inquire resource limitations, every light bulb will eventually go out, every water heater will eventually not heat, and every single wiring in the home will eventually short. Examine your transportation, your gas tank can only get but so full and your engine will only take you to a specific max of speed. Limitations create control and the control is incorporated into the development of programs. Hypothetically speaking, if your gas tank can only hold twenty gallons, you are only capable of paying for twenty gallons of gas usefully. Struggle is maintained by the limitations. Where you can go is determined by where you cannot go. Life appears free but that is only to the point that you are restricted from free will, to act on the thought of various other activities.

Summarizing this information, you can conclude with the idea that we are living in a society that permits us freedom to the program we can survive in. A janitor can and never possibly will have the congruent limitations as a lawyer. Schoolteachers will uncooperatively accept the annual salary permitting him or her to a necessity of consistent appearances in that labor field. They will have no other choice because that salary does not enable them to in a sudden act – stop teaching and take a vacation.

Have you ever heard someone say, '*I cannot afford a vacation?*' Most people respond by saying, '*You need to get a new job.*' Is it not obvious? Each program is only as apparent to what we selectively are willing to take on as a challenge to survive.

Merging Facts

We live amongst individuals who are born with a specific mental disability; we can use the expressive term "Mentally challenged." In other words, these individuals have minds malfunctioning to operate as what is supposedly known as normal. Several abilities such as thinking, reacting, choosing, playing, listening, speaking, crying, laughing, the use of emotions, and reading is either an action they cannot do or lack momentarily indefinitely. Those individuals diagnosed with symptoms that reflect the above absent abilities, have them by fate. They do not have an option to reverse, redevelop their life, or live without such significant powers. And, this is the incentive inspiring my irritated itch given by the label "Mentally Challenged." Shall we actually look at the word challenge from its book-defined perspective?

Challenge: A summon into contest or competition.

In order to make use of an effort or action, one would require the will to do so. In other words, the choice or option would be undeniably in favor. I see challenge as a word that means something may be an obstacle in any form of difficulty, which you can either get through or overcome. Competition involves an ending result with some sort of accomplishment. Contest is a term relatively of the same nature. A challenge contest or competition – can also be defined as tasks you have the capability of overcoming, by any and all means over time. So, how does an individual who lacks choice overcome, or perhaps, live with the tasks or challenge(s)?
How can anyone have the term – challenged – brought upon him or her, when the life they survive every day is designed with a permanent task. A mental impairment is developmental disability, and also recognized as any irregularity causing indefinite

fragmentary or absolute loss of operation within a body part, system, or organ. These my friends do not sound like there is an overturning result but tolerable contained circumstances. In other words, what we consider mental challenges are only mental disabilities. The real mental challenges are with those who live every day without any developmental disability or mental impairment to suffer from.

Every day because of the programs we all are inserted in, there are situations that involve survival challenges. These challenges are neither indefinite but rather temporary at the sake of our own will, whether our will leads to wise or obtuse intentions. Regardless, many of us have within and around us the power to overcome the very survival challenges that itch the soft spots of life. With the program at effect, the affect on us as a people and as individual's causes altered thought decision-making, overwhelming stress, and as well mental confusion that can result in the piling of every concern we have into one area of our minds.
Several other effects of the program can degrade one's thinking ability, causing challenges that will self-destruct the tolerance bomb keeping stress in its mental cage.
For years, we have failed to make choices that can benefit our future, which is why the challenges of the program arise so suddenly. However, when someone with autism suffers from immensely hindered communication skills, therefor their choices are highly limited as to what they could actually speak fluently on, it is very difficult to solve their personal issues. The capability and the useful act of speaking directly to address the issue, is not an option. Permanently.

More than enough factors bring us to approach the challenges that keep us in stress and struggling, which is after reflection causing the stress. The key to overcoming our challenges is not to live with them but get through them by taking them on. I will admit it takes a toll to run under the guidelines of the program uncomfortably and accept it as that, uncomfortable. Some of us suffer from different types of struggle and many become broken because of it. I am assuming health officials and doctors would say if you have no mental disability, you are pretty much normal. Our – us normal people - disabilities are beyond a tumor located on the corpus callossum, or an accompanying neurological disorder causing one's IQ score to classify us profoundly retarded. Are these true challenges?

How many single mothers have their license but no car? At that how many single mothers who have no money to keep a car if they had a vehicle, with their license?

What about the fathers who want to make an important career move to better their lives with their children, just to become bigger than the burdened stereotype. Unfortunate by far, the tasks we take on but mandatory at its most recognized relevance in survival. Another part of survival tasks, is love.

Love is a word that we use like it is a pick up line; everything brought with love is embedded in the mind, stored for its desired use when called upon. One of our hardest tasks is taking love and as it is summoned, using it for the designated purposes of the mind. Love is connected into the minds process by its presence as a beneficial quality. The mind is a tower with all the controls to function a person. The biggest and most beneficial qualities are in your mental remote. Thoughts are the channels – individual ones are containing many advertisements and episodes. Some run thoughts 24/7 while others may operate until a certain point, and then it goes into the paid program. Paid programs are the basic clockwork thinking. Our everyday thoughts are repetitive orderly to a continuous operation we often make an obstacle of (hence the idea of love as a task).

Mentally, the mind is used for what we allow it to process. Taking care of your mind is very imperative. Allow me with not only your given eyes – but the mind open to all information, welcome an understanding rejected irresponsibly. To set the title straight, the ones we should be labeling Mentally Challenged are ourselves. The responsibility of taken charge in our lives to overcome love concerns, program criterion, characteristic flaws and quality maintenance, and also the emotional reactions of one human to another; are all the challenges of the mind before they are concerns to the living world. By that fact alone, the challenges we suffer daily are consistent obstacles we take on repeatedly in our mind. Before we ever experience the next cycle of issues – being the obstacles repeating themselves – we oversee them from how we experienced them in our mind, then causing us to stress over those very obstacles before they even repeat due to the previous negative outcome. These are our mental challenges day in and day out. A strenuous tug from one thought to the other, our challenges are yet achievable while still improperly labeled. We are the mentally challenged.

Thinking

"If you don't respect my mind, you don't respect yourself, so why should I?"
- Ceazza Corleone

At the point we are responsible for actually thinking, we unfortunately find ourselves doing more reacting than applying our constant processed thoughts. Multitudes of situations will course the brain awaiting the point of acknowledgement. Several of these situations are easily described as our daily struggles; the daily struggles are mentally factored into our everyday lives and recognized as certain words, events, or visual preferences that are delivered actions to the brain before a single thought is created.

Waking up in the morning, you will perform actions that are first recognized due to information of not why to perform the action, but just the action itself being performed. Even, if the reason to perform any action is known to us, we do not consider thinking about the information, yet, instead we just omit it and process straight to the action.

For example:

In the morning you brush your teeth; before you made it out of the bed from waking up and all the way to the bathroom, you probably acknowledged the action but not the purpose of the act of brushing your teeth. Now you are saying "yeah, why not?" seems purposeless right?

WRONG

Consider the process – need it be particularly specific – you perform to brush your teeth. Brush top row, brush bottom row, gums, and then your tongue. Some of you brush your teeth in a motion to clean all of your teeth more thoroughly, while many of you probably slack off and do a mediocre brushing.

Imagine you wake up every morning and you begin thinking about the reason to brush your teeth. I mean you think about the negatives and positives all surrounding this dedicated process. Just thinking of the affect brushing your teeth can have on you will result in a few thoughts listed below:

1. You will begin to coincide how bad your teeth can become from lack of cleaning.
2. Knowing the consequences, you will make a far better teeth-cleaning experience, based upon the information contained while having negative thoughts of not brushing your teeth effectively.
3. You may actually begin new methods to ensure your teeth are being properly taken care of.
4. Just by thinking (THINKING) alone you have granted yourself the realization that you know why you should brush your teeth, and therefore you should continue to do so more consistent.

Thinking is a responsibility many of us are very remiss about when it comes to reflecting on our own thoughts, because so much can be taught mentally alone by simply thinking, our minds often take in all information presented. But, only we get to choose what stays. Thinking is an action we fail terribly at doing due to deficiency of time devoted to the active practice of actually doing it.

As we gather our thoughts, we will definitely process the positive thoughts but also we will process the negative thoughts even more. People are people, and through that truth alone, we are more than likely going to come to a negative vision and not allow how we feel – to become bothered by the thought of positivity controlling the outcome of our situations. Negative thoughts are worry factors, which bring in the mentally bad notions that stress the soul if considered repeatedly without control.

Due to these negative imaginations, the process of thinking or the idea of thinking is more choicely avoided. We imagine based upon experience and also expectation. Expectation is created from the mind remembering how it felt when a specific situation occurred. That situation – not necessarily primarily just yours – or anyone else's alone, is a diagram for your mind to follow. Chance and happening appear to enforce random and uncontrolled reactions, but are not designed to just force a straight reaction without any thought prior to the initiating situation. We by choice react without choice because we allow our minds to over look the diagram stored from every single situation. Making choices requires a very well maintained train of thought, and training yourself is a lot easier than just realizing what could have been prior to your reaction.

Every individual has choices, and whether we are fond of our decision-making skills, not one individual gives thought to choice by instinct. It is without instinct that we fail to think, as we fail to use a memory for its true purpose and not just some campfire story. We allow small concerns such as bad realizations in or out of a situation, to stop us from thinking. Thinking affects the performance and performance affects outcome and that will affect reality. Your reality is already predetermined by the diagram of your experience stored in thought, and this is why training your thoughts to seek what is already there is so effective.

As young adults, adults, and even elders, life has its pulls and pushes far greater than most imagine they struggle. We are living and breathing through tough and difficult days and will continue to until death, but regardless the obstacles involved in life's big rambunctious situations, THINK!

Various situations in life range from work, school, personal life, and relationships. Our decisions are "action decisions" and action decisions will only give us final results. In the world today, I highly doubt preparation before action would hurt us substantially. Before any presentation to your boss, or your class

CC

instructor in school, you would base your final results on prepared and thought out information, and not to mention studied and researched information as well. Thinking is preparation just as it is the practice before action and possibly the answer before question. The question is always asked after the results but only due to our failure to thoroughly review the situation. Questions after results should indicate to us that there should be incentive – new incentive, to find reason before action.

Basic life situations can easily be tackled with a choice of thought revision. At work, in your own home, or in any public area – thinking is a tool for action. In many of the angry atmosphere's we find it inevitable to walk into, the thought of thinking can be a bigger influence to find intention and persuasion to act before thinking.

We all have occupations where our bosses can intentionally attempt to jump on our case due to the fact they are just bad people who abuse their position of power. First things first, being the individual who is feeling bullied, you will then come to a boiling point and this point of anger is reached by the breaking of tolerance. Once our tolerance is broken we are pretty much loose cannons. The issue of broken tolerance transitions into a confrontation, and thus leads to us finding ourselves ready to lash out.

Most of us in the time of confrontation will lash out instead of preparing ourselves for the situation by thinking. For some of us, it results in losing our jobs as fast as we lose our temper. Really though, that's the motive! It happens that way because people of higher authority do not expect anyone below them to think. They expect you to provide you services through voice and command.

See the idea of us thinking is only needed when the task has been developed for us that way, otherwise the responsibility of thinking is least expected.

Thinking is the key to task completion and stability of operations within most businesses. No one wants you to think because the moment you do begin thinking, is the second you begin learning. Read the last sentence over. At a nine to five slave enforced occupation, do not shy away from the belief no one wants you learning. They want you to do what you are told, and that is where the operation of labor can deprive the mind that neglects thinking. The program is designed to keep us focused on certain responsibilities, that require us only being told what to do by the person above us in authority. If you have ever been at a job and asked someone of high authority how to take on a task, which requires full attention and directions to successfully complete the task – and run the task through. The powers that oversee do not want to tell you, and are not looking forward to a lower level employee using his brain for a job he is expected to shut up and just do whatever whenever told to do so.

Thinking is the part of life we are expected to abandon and leave on the streets of responsibility. All in all, we only abandon responsibility after we have ditched thinking. Ask yourself this, how do you learn from being irresponsible? You cannot and will not in a progressive state learn to move forward from being irresponsible at all, there is just no way. Irresponsibility causes you to hold yourself back while time progresses forward. Every mistake is made in the mind first before it ever sees physical evidence in reality. An act of irresponsibility is as severe as the thought, and both source the unintentional establishing act of procrastination. Procrastination is the mother of irresponsibility, which means time, must be the stepfather. Your time is the actual father in this illustration but not every biological father is responsible enough to watch over his seed. Metaphorically speaking, when a father does not take care of his responsibilities, he misses out on time to spend progressing with the growth out of procrastination.

Time wasted is exactly what many people need from you, some – those who are trying to help you, may find it offensive, yet others likely do not mind. The phrase goes, "Learn from your mistakes." Well that is exactly it, the time it takes for you to learn from your mistakes, is the time the people who want to make life harder for you, are counting on for you to waste.

You can bring yourself to the point where your brain wants to learn, and it becomes a tool used for the purpose of finding out what God wants you to do and not just daily, but for life. So many of us are drifting onto a path that has neither a title nor a position worthy to be followed. Your life can mean something, it is supposed to mean something and because we do not think, we act and move off of the worldly knowledge that keeps us running in this repetitive cycle – guiding us further from a path we are destined to venture.

Thinking is the reason you can and will overcome all obstacles brought your way. This is possible through the use of your brain to channel thoughts being constructed into actions. Allow yourself to accept the thoughts that come to mind in order to keep in touch with your actions. A paranoid schizophrenic may not or possibly may never have the opportunity to determine what thoughts are more valuable, at that sane over the others. If you are not thinking and are remaining in a lost world of do what you are told and ask no questions, you are no better than a paranoid schizophrenic, because you now have no choice to overcome any challenges. You will be systematically living with a disability. Many of us are aware enough to understand the life we live is organized outside our thinking. A program is keeping you entitled to the life others expect you to live, instead of the life you can choose to live willingly, as you synchronize your thoughts with your actions. To process a thought is as simple as moving one file from a folder to another. In this process, you must focus to select what thought best suits your capable action. Take thinking as an opportunity to jump out the window of reality and fly with your ambitions.

Life is best seen through the windows of reality, a window presenting us with the perfect opportunity to express our constant ability to think on an advance level. Thinking on an advanced level requires simple understanding of how to control your thoughts. This is a training process that you put your mind through, as you venture throughout the various ideas that surface every second of your living life. Training you mind begins when you allow yourself to consciously recognize a single thought on command. Kind of resembles the benefits of good memory, which is that moment you are asked about that specific event, with those specific people involved, and those specific details.

In time, you will understand what it means to control your thoughts. I say in time, because selectively grabbing a thought like a bear snatching salmon from the stream, is a bit task worthy. It takes you analyzing what matters to you most and sitting it aside, to take time to analyze what matters to others around you. What we do not factor into our consideration, is that what may often matter to others is our reaction and actions toward them. Knowing this is imperative due to the fact – and the only fact perhaps – you never know what you are doing to others because we are instinctively raised to protect ourselves. This protective demeanor instructs us to always review what is coming at us, and not what we are sending out. One of the first steps of training your mind will ask of you that you ignore your most inner feelings. Feelings without pause effect will seize ones attention so quickly that thinking of any other (for lack of better a word) moment, will be blocked out and one single thought attached to those feelings will be confined.

This is where you become the hero, at this point it is your inimical concern to break focus and create your own channel of focus on those things that are most deserted daily. Create a window by wanting to create a door, this window is the vision needed to find focus, and this is as relatable to looking through a window from outside of a house. You are searching to see if anyone is home and that is before you ever imagine the door you are locked out of is open. At that window, looking in is when your automatic focus is pin pointed onto what ever is in the house (your brain or that confined space). Control begins to feel more possible when you constantly remind yourself to stop looking in that window and turn around and look behind you. Behind you is a world of thoughts without any focus on them. Your moment to become ruler of your mind begins now! Take the initiative to aim at a certain thought and place definite focus onto it.

Think.

Choices

"The more precisely you plan. The harder
destiny will hit you."
- Ceazzar Corleone

"Disability – Mental or physical impairment, which depending on the degree, can hinder an individual's ability to independently complete daily and major life activities."

Choices

Choice is the keyword with a momentous definition that many of us have grown oblivious to. It is as if we intend to run through life off instinct and chance, and make no effort to enforce the idea of option. The gamble of life is living without choice and that is exactly how we are living, without it. Every mistake we make is an unknown area of fracture in our body of life, affecting us by the dormant results, which are rarely identifiable to a young life. We are always finding reasons in life to make decisions with our experience as a supporting reason after the fact. Often, we are taking the times of trials to be the reason we make any decision, yet, the reason disclose never justifies anything until after the event or incident, which your actions lacking choice, obviously have been displayed.

Seeking a reason is a way we make excuses for not using the choices we do have. We try to explain every action we make as if it were the key turning point to the conflict or alternating event we experience. Reality can make you believe everything is what is a fact, except what you can develop solely on your own as an opinion. It is remarkable how we stride through life with infinite careless attention to give to options available to us. Amazing how we have options to recognize and still take for granted the capability to identify them.

The road to understanding choice takes a bit of self-control and situation translation. We need to take away what would normally be defined or described by habitual behavior, and allow ourselves to see an open door of new opportunity through new maneuvers. The open door we seek is our moment of choice, and choice is a door that revolves universally. The idea of choice is less likely a thought we consider thinking before we react in any situation, which in fact is a sub-conscious choice in the making of making no choice at all.

Choice is the freedom to decide making a relevant optimistic decision based off evidence, which can provide you with an either/or as well as a neither/nor. The weight we place upon decision-making can scare any individual into just reacting. Think about it, when you consider the outcome, how often are you that willing to snap and act out of character to only realize later, you snapped and acted out of character. Imagine it to be instinct to begin to re-think steps and plan of action, just to keep in mind the reality of the consequences for any poorly made decision. With choice there is a consequence, however the consequences of choice are more favorable than we may recognize. Focus on the example a few sentences back; the one that focuses on snapping. Tourette Syndrome is best described by impetuous action or verbal movements such as – arm flapping; shoulder shrugging, or meteoric eye blinking, shricking, barking, outburst of incongruous words, and etc. This syndrome – Tourette's – is a bit tricky to relate to my point but it will serve a purpose in my presentation. With Tourette syndrome, snapping is quite the usual action. Hence, I used the word action because it is not likely to be the reaction as the condition is almost invariably constant. Not having such a condition appears to place us at an advantage and preserves our presence of choice. A stopped up nose is probably thee most annoying cold symptom, but envision that you had the sniffles and your primary care physician told you that you had them for life and cannot get rid of them. When you speak to people, you are sniffling throughout your conversation and they are not getting any comprehension of most of what you are trying to say. You do not have a choice to stop so you have to work around it, maybe write or pointing in hope you are understood. Such an involuntary behavior hinders you hopeless in a professional corporate world. The key point is that your snapping has no end and it is leaving you without choice. Lucky for you, you do not have the indefinite sniffles. Snapping is optional because you can stop to think and consider your next action.

Choice is the identity of option, the alternative way oppose to no way at all. Choice is also universal and can be created, developed, constructed, planned, and re-enforced. The worst result making a choice can bring is the realization that you had a choice and are still negligent to the obvious. Therefore, if one can be as careless to accept the obvious outcome, he or she may deserve every consequence a poor choice can provide.

We toy with the chances in life when choice has no significant existence in our daily lives. People say they live for today — as you should in a manner of speaking — as we move towards the un-promised future in tomorrow. And, just like that my argument is would not living for today, be taking a chance at trusting in the idea there may be no tomorrow, and if so, chance has no choice because you are logically living with no options.
Everyone needs choice, it is a blessing that God has given to us even knowing what we will already do and how we will do it.

Choice is going to, if you allow it to — keep you on the road you belong on, and can and will if used incorrectly keep you on a road that has many signs warning you there is construction work ahead. Worst of all cases in not acknowledging we have a choice, is that some of us become leaders of a blind society. Many individuals begin to seek the knowledge illustrating how to become an individual who has no choice, which are typically the actions of today we find delight in entertaining. Choice is the profit of living, and the life you choose to live as well as how you live it will best fit your life comfortably.

Many of us today are living without a choice and allowing what appears obligated to determine the choices we have, kind of like the sniffles. Several of us get up for work or school and decide nothing because we act as if the decision has already been made for us. It is the situations in our lives that prove choice cannot be controlled, realizing that may be the reverse psychology needed to turn time into your favor. Living is a pattern many of us construct mentally perfectly, with expectations we pray upon to be revealed as we display our actions. The issue of life, appearing controlled – forms when the life we live brings us more problems with every choice we are with great ignorance making.

Solutions brought by God are apart of choice, and the conflicting results in any situation are brought upon by the devil in thought. Although, God already has our lives mapped and predicted, so choice is a blessing he gave to us with intuition. God wants to know if you are going to follow through with the choices of his provision. By simply ignoring God's set in place decision-making moments, you leave yourself vulnerable to the sniffles type of lifestyle. The part of Tourette's Syndrome that is significant to this chapter is the idea that controlled actions will have no choices. Without choice, well there simply is no challenge. Choose is what you have to do and will do regardless and forever.

Consistent are we to step out of the house with what we have known for the longest as "Proper" traditions of presenting your attitude, clothing yourself, and eating. Every single little step in this designed life has its own program and direction. As these programs – uninterrupted – persist in process, we follow them without an option we have. The responsibility is only ours as a body of people and individuals to be aware of the living patterns that we accept, and also allow to bring us the absence of choice we believe we have.

Ask yourself, have you allowed waking up and going to work make the day for you?

Let me ask you another question, what happens on that day you wake up and say I am not going to work? Do you not go? Do you go?

Alternatively, because of the choices you do not believe you have, you will already before the answer of the question can even be decided begin to start the no choice speech that begins with these questions. Who is going to pay the bills? How will the bills get paid? How will I keep a roof over my head?

No one is asking you to quit your job, and if you like your job stay there, have fun, and be bossed around. For those who do not want to live their life being bossed around, and trust me there is a very enormous amount of your kind who does not because you all complain about your jobs. You all come home or gather around groups of friends, sit down, and open up the book to read to your pity party. Violins please.

Suck it up, there is no one to blame but you for not realizing you have a choice or choices. Our eyes cannot always see the options on the table, and our eyes may never see options at all. On the other hand, having practically a choice is visually abroad. First, open your mind and think, we are allowing bills and various other pity concerns to keep us in programmed living systems while without choice. Most of us go to work and some of us get promoted inside the work force. Some of us get promoted externally by transferring to another occupation with greater priorities. Regardless, the reason we all keep our jobs is because we do it either very well noticeably or very terribly unnoticeably.

The occupation that you choose to suffer from comes back at you ten times harder by the day you go without thinking and becoming aware of choice. Now don't you find it funny how we can always know what we are suppose to do, but, when it boils down to doing it almost anything can distract us from doing so. Ironic being as though it never works like that with our lives, we never just know we are supposed to go to work and get distracted by something else that interest us. Only when we are at a minor focus of interest does the choice to keep focused and continue or ditch the priority, lead to following the interest. Choice is going to haunt many of us as it already does. Several of you are reading this and many of you can stop, sit back or look up, and say something about at least five decisions you have made on your path and find some disgust to them as you ask yourself, why.

"Omg why did I do that..." sound familiar...

Yes, that is you sounding all regretful and just lost in the midst of your uncontrollable sniffling. Pssh so...
You have choices in this present day, and whether you believe it or not, your choices are going to be more of a positive burden than a child would. (Hence the fact your lack of choices bring children into this world)

Problems are what we decide they are and they are at times the solutions from many choices. Decisions are crucial and imperative to the time line of life and the rebuilding of character. We will list the clear facts of struggle and dependents that will keep us surrounded by a reality, which we only construct from slacking between our thinking. Mentally we are built to learn and the mind can never go far from learning right when a choice is at stake. Mistakes will be made and we know this because our actions display our mistakes every day. Examples of our character are reactions

CC

based off actions displaying the choices acting as a sphere around our reality. The most unimaginable of our thoughts are the possibility to find the choices useable. The argument will be stated but the realization will be absent. Here you walk into the open arms of acknowledgment and recognize that choice is power, and also a tool. The will to act on choice is also a blessing in disguise greater than fathomed.

Open eyes of folly competitors will look past the silver and shoot for the platinum, as its shine is far brighter and obvious. Little do we understand, the choice of platinum over silver – wanting the first thought that comes to mind, is over a little foolish interest in trained appeal. The more we continue to put ourselves in the position to be without choice, the pain and struggle of living is never going to be understandable with it.

Become the dominant determiner in your life after God's will has been set and discovered. Our choices will bring us so much realization that the world around us will be unveiled from the dark shade it places over us, putting us in a place we cannot function on our own. It begins to unfold as the days of living with a choice become more non-negotiable. When you have applied so much of your life into what you thought you were suppose to do, you will live with the type of regret the sniffles will only remind you of forever.

The mind is the starter of all decisions, and in the mind you are either susceptible or dominant in regards to choice. Do not allow the ways of the mislead mind to mislead you into a life challenged by falsified beliefs. You are so powerful when you understand choice and how having it can no longer be a challenge when you accept its existence. Reality is more than the lies based on the myths produced from the ideas of freedom. Uncontrolled actions have no reactions. Remember this, as time shall reveal that choice is a

challenge best acknowledged in the mind of one
confident with accepting his flaws. Accept your
disability, your hindered actions are due to your
challenge of lack of psychological will towards
acknowledging that you have a choice.

Talent is Talent

The creativity to obtain an objective and selectively create a method, which not only proves to dominate the core responsibility of the objective, but as well mark the specific criteria of the solutions, is a gift beyond. Some of us can fly a plane while others can operate a U.S. military tank. Using process of elimination or even the mathematical equations we all grow to despise in math class, as we establish an understanding that advances any noun in its primary state to a secondary state – but not inferior to – is idiosyncratic. While many skills of the world are publicly known, there are various types of unidentified crafts that build our constant developing character. In the position under the spotlight, the shine can take a mind to a place called "confidence." The confidence you can establish from the desire to be in the position to be seen as successful will ensure that you are beginning the right path with determination in mind.

Determination is one of many keys to becoming what talent defines. The reason a talent is magnificent is because of its use with the act of determination. Creating an ideal location in your mind and life to set a goal is one of the beginning steps in establishing determination and drive, and with that said talent could be any skill fueled by determination. Learning to build on determination is first supported by the will to explore with your talent and with the intent to become confident in expressing what exactly your talent is.

Now, you may ask, "Cori, well why and how is this a mental challenge?"

Well, it could not be a misunderstanding capable of re-enforced information neither a broad casting display of ignorance, or it could be both.

Today, we are labeling our actions and decisions too far off, even to determine what is effective and what will be effective. The soul of desperation has become

CC

the cruel body of selective imperfection. Minds have isolated specific procedures used for transferring information, and detailed actions, into the realization of our own public eyes. No longer are we carrying an eye for interest any more than we are wearing Prada for skin comfort. In fact, we are just scoping the scene for non-extraordinary but regular identical interest.

The facts of the last sentence will soon stand out as obvious as the fact; our nations first black president is being targeted by identical interest in public grouping speculators. Nonetheless, talent is talent and to have the capability to do anything that others have to learn, or even create an understanding of how you are capable of doing what it is you can do, is also what we call a natural born talent. As more concerns for the skilled leaders of the country hit the lecture board, you can never fully prosper with the skills presently expressed, due to the fact those in charge are not searching for extraordinary, which leaves you unwanted in the Light of Command.

Light of command is the point of position where you have skillful exposure at the breaking point within your ability to control. By breaking point, I insist that you have the ability to maintain influence on your actions verbally, physically, and mentally within the act of your actions. Skill is highly over looked now and days, and especially if your skill is far from what the identical interest speculators sees as an opposite. How could skills be seen as an opposite?

The facts stand long and aloud, there are several talented individuals – but without Light of Command as a resourceful insight, which leaves the talent without relevance placed into a category I call Who Cares?

Who cares?

No one will care when the talent you have is not of his or her (those in charge) nature. The extraordinary skill is a talent speaking from its displayed expression, and also reminds you of many capabilities we can be ignorant to. Together, we have become our own disregarding counterpart in the process of nit picking what is considered skill or talent. One thing worse than being told you have no talent is to disregard your own talent with your own disbelief.

Let us be realistic, anything can be a talent. There are so many creative minds living and breathing with well-constructed methods and alternative acting creativity. The capability to act upon the knowledge of a classical talent or skill is by all means possible. However, the sad part is we are allowing ourselves to over look our own skill, but why?

The overlooking of our self-developed talent is due to what we know or at least are being informed to know. Look at today's living patterns and exchanges; nothing you can do uniquely is being brought to the table as a talent. They have exploited so much of our relevant tasks and creations that the displaying of them almost appears to be nothing new. Intellectually, we are far greater and smarter than some simple designed plan to keep those who are picked into success to be the only ones who are bound for success.

Ready the ears and eyes for this message comes very swiftly. Your ability to create, discover, and operate is what defines your talent as one. Issues with this identity are that they have no interest in your direction you see with your talent, because you are not what they can identify as their interesting perception of greatness.

See the world seems so full of everything that it is clearly impossible to stand out and the reason is they do not want you to. If you review back a couple paragraphs, I mentioned the "Light of Command," which plays an important role in living and operating amongst those power junkies, who are in control of how difficult it can be for you to become successful. Power junky leaders have created a forceful lock down system on what will be talent-exposed talent, and then determined as talent in conclusion. It will appear as if

CC

there is nothing new about your particular skill-set, due to the infatuation with power and those with it being capable of identifying how your skills can bring them more power. Take celebrities for example and the correlating relationship to their fans. Celebrity's fans love them and love to see them as much as they love to cry for them, learn about them, laugh about them, support them, and establish a clear understanding about them. One thing that you may notice about talent in the spotlight is the talent owner has control i.e. power. Use musical artist for example, people come to see a musical figure display their talent openly, and due to what that talent can bring you, it inspires you to feel connected. People want inspiration and inspiration builds the connection of ear to mouth control. Now, at a concert if the musician said everybody jump and put your middle fingers up, everyone will do it because the position of an artist words creates trust – between the listener – using the feeling created through music as the identity of chemistry. And this exposure allows talented publicized individuals to obtain control over their listeners.

Many of us will find that because the obstacles have been pre-set, we are incapable of seeking out the goals we have placed our aim on. The same way artist make a connection with their fans, power leaders use a marketing system they can control to give you the impression that what they advertise is talent. It is the connectivity of you being persuaded with glamour glorifying a specific skill, which is flavored down to create an artificial influenced interest.

I know a young man, who suffers from Attention Deficit Hyperactivity Disorder and he is very observing and has skilled hearing. His work ethic is incomparable and before I begin working with him I sensed an energy that produced positive vibes. He was and possibly today still is famous for less forgiving acts, although I read over this guy's paper work I didn't feel any pre-cautionary advising from my instinct. What stood out about this man was his ability to care. I truly

believe this guy had a talent for caring, I am talking if
he can help he would help but he always knew who to
help. His disability played into his actions many times as
we met on and off. Several times he'd make decisions
that didn't reflect any choice or lack of any thought to
the outcome. It bothered me most that even after such
occurrences, this guy's positivity would click on like clap
on lights. At any instant, he would review exactly a
situation of misfortune and deal with it. To me it
appeared he was the sinner who sinned and would
repent with his actions.

    One day, a few guys with us where out of cash,
he didn't know they were at a lost but someone how
throughout the entire day, he managed out of his
personal lunch box and seven dollars to help all three of
the guys get breakfast and lunch for the day. They
never asked, which was the amazing part. It was like he
knew that day he needed to share or help out. At first, I
thought wow cool guy, but it happened over and over
periodically. Over the course of five months, whenever
one or two of the three guys had no money, this guy
was on it. He just offered so much on those specific
days only without a clue; I mean no one told him prior.
It did not stop at money, as over the same course of
time he would talk to them and make major efforts to
cheer them up, if one was less communicative or
frowned with no intention to break face. Strangers were
now accomplices to his acts of genuine kindness. For
the most part, I couldn't tell if I was meeting the most
conflicting form of an angel, who had not realized he
was an angel and happened to sin very often.

    Many of you can get something different from
this, but I tell you from my own experience, it was a
skill and appeared to reflect a natural emotional effort,
to sense the connectivity of feelings or demeanor
coming from the people who surrounded him. I share
this experience to say it doesn't matter who you are and
what your considered condition or situation is, talent is
talent. The titles we place on many of the individuals
with exploited talent in a way places this unknown

CC

limitation to the exploitation of other career making talents. This guy I described could possibly work in a multiple number of fields due to his connection with other people. Those who govern over his activity actually hinder him because of his disability. The challenge to recognize here is that we can be crippled by the every day alternating particular skills, which are only being brought to us as the primary identification of a skill that is beneficial in life.

Talent is, or, at least should be the core of your determination, and also a high contributing factor into the outcome of what you will more than likely decide to do with your life. We cannot continue to see what others do as a talent as a competitive angle of offense. Everyone is born with a unique talent, even some individuals, and the same talent for a better connection to help others in a relevant field – of their own – with the practicing of perfection of their talent. A passion you develop for a craft can develop a path of success with inspiration encouraged into the purpose. Allow talent to become seen for what it is and will be, talent.

After all talent is talent.

Part-time

Using your ability to focus, thinking of creative ways to make a difference from the normal way things are – like the way things can be done, how they will be done, and what inspires the will to do it – is often made useful by thinkers who focus on the variety of methods to perform any task. Our brains think of ways to change what we see most interest in changing, and this is a constant sub-conscious approach to advancing from one state of living to the next. This interest in change keeps the eye surrounding the topic of such with ideas, which helps determine a more useful form of change. Change benefits those who act off of a change and not those who expect change to make everything in life react as a result of it. Sadly, it does not work to sit and wait for the effects of change, especially when change is only useful as a reaction.

From here, I assume you get my point, which is change really does not alter anything that we do not act on ourselves to invest in. You may wonder what topic I am about to investigate, well my dear letter lovers I will be discussing change without self-reaction to change existing very strongly in the work force.

Who are the ones that suffer this extreme undergoing of not making constructive efforts to see better results of change?

Part-time workers.

Yes, part-time employees are being challenged every day at work and do not even understand how. Part-time, and first let us become familiar with part-time employment and exactly what failure to react to change they suffer from.

Part Time:
  ◆ Part-time employees cannot work more than 40 hours per week.
  ◆ Have no benefits in regards to health, dental, visual, or etc.

✦ Rights of the job are that you have a job and are expected to appreciate it.

    ✦ Internal benefits of the job are you get a fifteen-minute lunch break.

    ✦ Part-time employees cannot advance to any position of authority, thus lacking in the amelioration of leadership.

    ✦ Part-time employees are to do as instructed and if instructions are questioned, a higher authority challenges them.

    ✦ Salary is just enough to make sure you have lunch money to buy a happy meal every day from McDonalds.

    ✦ Part-time employees receive no bonuses regardless of full effort applied to the completion of their task.

    ✦ Part-time employees are responsible for coming to work at an assigned time, where as though anyone else who is not part-time, will not be monitored as heavily for tardiness while still responsible for the identical assigned time.

    ✦ Part-time employees will have a chain of command above them that drops them to the very bottom of the list

    ✦ No one appreciates the work ethic of part-time employees but only observes such ethic to ensure the part-time work is completed.

So what exactly is part-time employment for?

I would like to develop an idea in my own mind, which is part-time employment falls under the re-developing motives designed to give students a chance to make some income, and as well gain working experience at an early age. So, if I am correct on this idea, then why are there not students enrolled in office working part-time. Interns are what they call the college graduates or possible current enrolled students – who are associated in a program in the company, but are not currently employed by that company. Now in office, there may be contract employees and they are the idea of seasonal or part-time employees in other organizations. But, why are there no actual part-time jobs in office, and then again does it matter?

The idea runs around my brain like my thoughts are a track meet, and it is like a question I have competing with speculated concerns to gain full understanding of how a powerful country allows its own to suffer.

When do we acknowledge this, and if acknowledged why do we accept it?

Programs developed for your survival are responsible for the way you live when you allow higher powers to choose them for you. Working a part-time job is supposed to establish experience within the working systems of labor, develop knowledge surrounding the areas of a certain skill or expert position, and gain the full understanding of how to live life accepting you have to work at a job set to pay you by hours. Employment as part-time should only be used to develop laboring skills capable of helping one advance into greater areas of employment. Imagine the orientation and pre-development classes you go through before your exact start date of employment. Part-time work is like the training you get paid for and experience to say I have been there and done that.

My question is, why do adults and elders who have lived through experiences exhibiting dreadful struggles, have to now appreciate the opportunities in part-time employment? I do not know if you are aware but babies are dropping from the sky like rain. The responsibilities to provide substantially for another human being are being issued at an irrepressible rate. People need to be able to provide for their families but not just on the line separating barely capable from fairly capable. Companies who present full-time employment opportunities are subjecting applicants to becoming employed by part-time laborers due to such repudiation rates. It makes sense to say this fact is a contributing factor and reason poverty is a big deal in America.

If we analyze this information, adults above the ages of nineteen are receiving part time positions and sustaining these positions in similar appreciation to full-time employment. As of today, there is a 34.7% rate of birth per 1,000 girls aged 16 through 21. Now, not only that but check out this researched information, which states of the youth at least 50% become pregnant before the age of twenty.

WOW!

A detonating fact revealing you have parents who are attempting to provide for parents on part-time salaries. Not only are they trying to provide for parents, but also they have to do it on part-time benefits and pay, which I announce again. I cannot accurately numerate the amount of part-time employees in America. Teenage parents are competing with their elders and parents to find employment in the same labor title. If you have ever been to a group interview or orientation, you will notice there are all ages applying for a variety of part-time positions.

Although, look at it this way – there are more people who need to keep a company running where there is money generated, than people needed to say one word or sign papers to make sure the business in general stands.

What does this mean? There is nine times out of ten only one CEO, more than likely several hundreds of managers and presidents, rare chiefs and executives, and over hundreds of thousands of full-time employees possibly even millions. Where do you think the average numbers for part-time employment may fall?

I suggesting somewhere in the billions but I could be wrong, no wait – 8.613 million people in 2012 are statistically recorded as part-time employees in the U.S. alone. If we attempt to estimate a fraction of those employees – across the United States – who have children who have children, I am going to round my percentage to let's say 63% of that 8.6 mil. Flip a page or two back and you will see the description for part-time employment above. People, if we can put two and two together from the list; the 65% estimate of parents with children who are parents – do you honestly believe these families are making enough and gaining enough support from their jobs that they can provide for their families.

The work force has become a chain of destruction leaving the struggle to affect millions of people, who strive to survive, and even as they do the times are going to get harder and the stress will become constant. Wake up, because nothing is changing for you and you have to make the changes you want now. As vital functions change you have to react to them as they do, due to the changes only benefitting you when you do react. We are going out chasing job after job but are not even making a set amount of funds efficient enough to survive, and now the goal is converted to make any income capably accessible.

Some of us are working two part-time jobs, which the money appears ok because it comes in more frequent. In all actuality, two part-time jobs are two negative positions producing the façade of one whole financial benefit. You are working two jobs and will receive no benefits from either occupation; as well obviously you cannot work more than forty hours a week because if you do, you might just make enough income to control your bill payments every month. Do not play with life because it is not a game and people are struggling without hope. Working two part-time jobs as an adult or elder is a practical survival game.

The employment business is complicated, and it is designed with no particular interest in employees developing themselves with the knowledge an occupational industry can offer. Labor is designed to provide a balance of programs that can keep order in a far sight view of authority. Programs are designed for every class of financial income and we are marked with our labor and tracked by our measurable income i.e. taxes. The road to success is not a part-time experience and neither is it full-time, but you can be comfortable by means of interest and desire to do what you feel is best in your capabilities. Most jobs are not going to offer you a chance to display a powerful talent, which can serve a greater purpose and display a more evident worth. Highly unfortunate, but the obligations are set in stone like the sword Excalibur, and the rules are made like commandments. Part-time employments are a listen and follow organization and no one gets to lead but the designated leaders.

No leader will lead himself if being lead in a chain of command he cannot find the floor to have a voice in. Working in part-time, you are the bottom of the bucket and you are the last option to be considered a valuable option for any profitable incentive. You are significant by means of keeping an operation progressing doing exactly what bushel of tasks are required of you to see through. There is no goal for your position neither is there advancement, so if you are an elder who is taking care of children taking care of children, you can imagine how bad the struggle is for this sort of labor. Teenage parents have to compete with there own parents to get a part-time job, which let's us know that students college and high school are not getting any labor experience. By the time students reach an age where a full-time job is only acceptable for sustaining any standard of living, they'll have no prior working experience, and thus are now competing with elders who do – to get jobs they are over qualified for.

Realize, I am telling you we are all challenged due to our lack of thinking proficiency in knowing our strengths as individuals and as well having faith in them. We are settling for what is there and refuse to chase what is definitely out there for the opportune taking. How many of my readers are working two part-time jobs? How many of you are working one part-time and one full-time job?

You are working two jobs because you have bills you need to pay now, and one part-time occupation is not giving you enough to get by 25% of your financial responsibilities. Yet, neither is one full-time occupation assisting you in encouraging 25% into the minimum 75%. At these two part-time or part-time/full-time jobs, you are struggling not just financially but as well mentally. This consciousness leaves you where in life at this moment? You are practically stuck, and with no direction but that same old voice in your head telling you what you intend to do but are not doing.

Why are you remaining a victim to the challenge of understanding yourself productively? With statistics like those stated above and pure logical connecting facts, now is the time to use what will power you have to initiate some mental form of battle strategy. Living today is a mental war and every thought that slips into the beliefs of societies logical way of living, is another soldier gunned down. Make no mistake in believing that employment is impossible to re-peak. Just like there are millionaires, it is also involved with the fact a portion of their gross income goes out to the employees servicing the customers that earn them such a banner.

Focus on what is really going on here; some are misfortunate enough – unable to overcome the fight to be in the position to decide an occupation. There are individuals with disabilities that keep them from ever knowing what it is like to use something they are talented at to finance their life. Programs are set, and in motion, while steering those who submit to the criterion presented in the programs, into a sphere of soon to be unbreakable barriers.

You are full of many talents, and many only you will distinguish as a gift, yet no other individual may be cognizant of your ingenuity even in the presence of you displaying it. Grow conscious of your blessed talent and train to become comfortable with it – placing the beauty of its results into the definition of your life. Stop falling for what seems apparent and financially accessible but is perniciously unprogressive. To mothers and fathers, as well as all individuals upholding responsibility as a parent, think about what we pay for infant and toddler necessities and how part-time work contributes to the salubrious living patterns. Mandatory requirements for an infant and toddler to undergo minimum level proper care can be and are very costly. Which is completely outrageous – being as though we make these claims of child abuse, negligence in parenting, and that parents are not suitable for their own children, when majority of the time those unfit to care for a child have to pay for taking care of one. Irony.

They have developed W.I.C, which basically is a front of money to help under paid or no income parents attain the requirements of an infant or toddler. For every effort to organize vouchers and send out contained materials, why is it not free? Why is baby food a costly item? Ok, some edible essentials for a child goes as low as a dollar, but after you calculate the amount needed you are already looking at twenty dollars spent for baby food in one grocery outing. Make nutriments free if taking care of infants/toddlers is that important to America. At this time and day it is obvious that some parents are not going to be able to take care of their children, and this is due to the part-time income they struggle to flex throughout by-weekly pay periods.

Understand, you are being forced into the by laws of a program every day this program exist. They have the resources but monitor how those resources are distributed, but with the monetary system our nation is being governed under, it is mandatory the system persist in order to generate a flow of incoming and outgoing revenue. You are kicking out money but for different reasons than your government desires. You want to feed and secure the survival of your child, however, the government wants you to support a system that is deemed necessary to encourage growth and survival, all while hindering you from providing life sustaining essentials definitely. My dear friends, we are being ruled over.

MAKE IT FREE!

Connections made to the references above will show with the requirements of designated money locations, and the established programs designed to keep you employed in part-time occupations, you are being challenged to survive. The distinctive difference between us – who have not been diagnosed with a mental disability, and then those individuals who are, is we can become prematurely and maturely coherent with the forces against us. The benefits of part-time employment have been disclose to you, the facts tell you all about the jobs you are getting into and how your struggle is designed with no greater achievement than preserving your struggle constantly. Why short yourselves of your talents and comfortable living for what seems like the door to a way out of no way?

If you haven't noticed yet, I am asking questions but not answering them. This chapter is called part-time, now do your job full-time and fight the challenge.

Factors to consider

1. Being a man holds pride to limits, self-esteem to cockiness, ambition to greed, power to domination, emotions to cease existence, understanding how to be misunderstood, being misunderstood with an understanding, faith without fear, impression with a stereotype, attraction to satisfaction, bold to bravery, intelligence and wisdom, right and wrong, and an image to define displaying it all.

2. Today, love is not holding the same definition it held fifteen to twenty-five years ago. Love is not an emotion by societies present classification, yet, neither a considerate element of feeling. Love is a word that bares desires and not needs, not understanding, and neither compromise. The word love has lost its meaning because today we use every single quality and critiquing characteristic – to physically construct what pity of feelings we intentionally insult love with. These feelings navigate to money, cars, clothes, living patterns and routines, appearance, popularity contest, and recognition for any reason explaining someone's evident presence.

Only after do we actually consider the small concerns for ones personality. Ladies, ever wonder why you meet a man who has it all and he still hits you right in the face to the point of anger, and this is with his mislead truth and not so truthfully careless behavior. Fellas are you still wondering why women will use and abuse the benefits you work and earn, and this is with no regard for the hard work you put in to earn them. Men and women lie and insult each others values for trust and respect.

Here let me introduce you to some of the ideas why: -Money -Cars - Clothes

-Living patterns -Appearance

-Popularity
-Recognition

Read them and learn them until you understand them. When you find someone you like it will be the only reason your eyes and emotions will be able to touch them. Personality is a flaw first and interest second. With that said, I suggest we stop looking for what is obviously seen over what can be timely recognized.

3. Parents are the burden of their children. If you do not appoint your child's life in the direction where they will see opportunity, they will suffer. Your children are the product of you, the living example of your accomplishments and achievements. I don't care if your parents were on crack, financially challenged, deadbeat and out of your life, or even unsupportive. Do not send your children through your struggle, they did not ask for it and damn sure do not deserve it. Position is everything in a child's life and our youth struggle because we allow it. Do what you have to do and stop ending another person's future before they even have a chance to begin it. No child should struggle to find the opportunities through food, shelter, clothes, school, transportation, or work. Nine out of ten teens I have reached out to, I found they are ill informed by their parents. They are either not informed or under the same morals of their parents struggle, which is completely unfair. I do not care about what you went through or if you had every problem in the world, strap onto your faith ship and talk to God so you can change your child's life. It is not fair and more than un-called for that your children suffer from your misfortune and lack of will power to enforce the reality of a better capable future for them. Pursuing this future with low or high interest can build a chain of failure or success. You are the first link in this chain and it is imperative you become aware of that. You have every opportunity

CC

to make your children something remarkable. This is the last generation where our youth become mislead by ignorance in the household. Make a change.

4. Actions speak louder than words, and if so, we can have these talks about our government and we can discuss over and over the disabilities of our country. We can anger ourselves over Americas so free country while baring the most controlling restrictions. However, I must say if you are going to speak up then speak up. Every government building, agency, corporation, program, and organization has a phone number, become the government's bill collector. Google the contact info and speak your mind as clearly as the words can sound from you dissatisfied lips. As a body of people who represent our America it is our obligation to speak. As much as we discuss our problems and concerns on a daily living basis through social networks and blogs, why not speak your opinion where your opinion will be heard by those who do not share the same concerns, or particularly care to hear them.

Every government has a mailing address and that makes speaking your mind now the task and challenge. For we are citizens of a country that demands to control our lives daily and they do not fear us, therefore we shall make those moves and take those steps they ever so carelessly doubt we will ever make.

Factors to consider...

Parenting

"We want to only focus on positives, but you may never see the positives you install in your child at a young age, sometimes the result of a good teaching go unseen. It does not always mean what was taught to your child did not get applied."

– Tony

The Parent

Please try to understand as parents your job is full of responsibilities, which in most cases are directly integrated into the systems of life as routines. I am speaking in reference to all whom are parents and legal guardians. The time to find legible reason in carrying out our responsibilities as parental leaders is now. There is a mental disruption that has brought parenting to a misfortunate and convoluted ideal process. As parents it appears we are mentally confused with the idea of having children and raising them to be productive and successful as they grow into becoming young adults. Of course, what we wish for and want from all of our children is classified as the best outcome but also requires the best of our efforts.

When it comes to raising children, many parents are running off of the idea that you commonly have to feed and keep a roof over your child's head. This is in fact not at all wrong, however, it is also merely a contribution to parenting. Knowledge is the key and it will always keep a door open on this earth for as long as it exists. Learning is an action so powerful it determines how you live, act, and respond to the world. Information is a tool of life – capable of assisting the fixture of any broken dream due to its consistent and immense extensibility.

Our children need to know doors of opportunity are out there, and while finding them due to untimely obstacles may be a bit impractical, youth need to be knowledgeable in all areas of life where learning is capable. As parents, you provide food and shelter, clothes, shoes, and personal essentials. With these essentials, we rely on to guide our children to school, work, and life, these essentials are also leaving their minds empty and without common sense or wisdom.

You may have found that even kids who have had doors of opportunity opened at an early age, still have grown within the midst of failure. Money flooding the lives of certain teens has still become the definition of corruption and ignorance in the lives of the youth. This is due to the ignorance our children inhabit leaving them oblivious to what information can be learned – coincidentally while they are surrounded by information.

The most hidden yet obvious eager addiction within our young but growing human beings is to know. The idea for most youth is to know any information that they do not currently know pertaining to their interest. Students of society hunger to know about music, fashion, money, and other glamour's in life. Misleading life instructions are bringing the minds of our youth to a halt on what they need to know, opposing to what they can know and how they should know it. What is worst is the problem thickening when the youth begin to teach themselves; the life they are being exposed to, becomes the psychological failing deviant. As parents, the advantages and disadvantages of teaching our children vary with us all, but this is not the problem to the system of parenting. Every child should and must know the possibilities of learning. Learning is the leading cause of adults who can control their outcome as an individual trying to survive. Individuals with knowledge, which has been attained and earned, comprehend complicated misunderstandings of laws and regulations.

Some of you are staring at this paper directly at the beginning of this sentence and ask yourself, learning? Next, you are saying learning is not the only problem with parenting. Of course learning is not the only problem with parenting but it is a pretty big ass problem contributing to the flaws in the process.

Learning is in fact the issue and if you feel differently, how well is your child coming along? Lie to me, lie to these pages, and share your lies with other readers, but you cannot lie to God. It is important that

CC

learning is enforced into the every day routines of our children's lives. Learning is the optimal option dividing failure from success. Honestly, the realistic connection between school and general public life is the act of learning. Our children are not learning and will continue to neglect learning as long as we are not teaching them to understand the process, to like the process, and become sensible of the benefits. The time to make a difference is now and with the doors of opportunity narrowing down as our youth progress into new experiences.

Schools have become optional – obviously now, and in the past years public or private school's have had optional existence, in reference to students knowing their responsibility of attending school. If you question me about this drastic statement then my answer will remarkably shock you into an understanding you will fight to change.

Our children get up morning after morning and are walking into classrooms like some mind controlled beings mentally being forced to go in and sit and learn. Realistically, our children reach school systems and are deciding themselves what they will learn. Which if you think about it is not straight away a bad idea, but that is until you consider what they are choosing to learn on their own without pre-invested knowledge from their parents. Many of our youth are going to school and are choosing to learn about topics school systems do not even educate students on. Drugs, sex, fashion, music, cars, and various other frivolous activities – which involve all the previous topics – are all that students are choosing to educate themselves with. Teens are choosing to learn inadequately inside school systems, and what they choose to learn in the school system is optional but falsified concerns that have been given grand attention in society. Teachers are going to do their job to the best of their capabilities and administrators will conduct rules and regulations as required to maintain campus stability. However, school employees' doing their job does not embed useful information into the student body and neither does that make information any more easily accessible in schools.

You will have students who will come in and learn as instructed and are knowledgeable of their decision to take in constructive information. They are part of a small percentage of teens that are processing thought selection – while prematurely – still positively and aware enough to see benefits in the school system. Some will go to school and learn because it is what they feel as though they are supposed to do and will not question why they are supposed to do it. There is also a percentage of students who will teach themselves and are in the classrooms being the teachers of their own demise – as lack of parenting does definitely.

In these classrooms students are informing themselves with the information they best see fit due to their ignorance within questionable areas in school education. Behavior from these students exceeds unacceptable as teens are choosing to learn from the most misleading sources of information, which is psychologically persuading them to act combatively. Once the school doors open and the bell sounds, it is a different world for children blundered with the reoccurring non-existing acts of parenting. Students are in the hallways experiencing their youth life without a concrete knowledge, exposure to any form of labor, and life without bills and identifiable priorities. The students are just free and to them school can be the door to freedom or the hell from heaven, this depending on how well they are being coached to absorb knowledge. Heaven being home, imagine what student wants to go to school and focus on learning with the insults and grief as an under privilege child. Self-destruction begins in the early teen years, and the booming explosion of harsh criticism and motivation deprivation is the moment they begin walking the path deviating from chances of seeing a beneficial future.

As parents we have to take the initiative to set the fields of learning as wide as possible. Raising a child is not easy and can become fairly difficult as children progress in age. One of the most difficult practices for a parent is to teach, and as parents we are mentally challenged to teach our own children. The strength it takes to actually become an influential figure by attaining knowledge capable of being redistributed, is astounding. It is okay to reach out and learn and become an educational factor in your child's life.

There are parents out here who can barely read, some speak, and pronounce words correctly. Many parents are uneducated and negligent to the educating process their own children undergo. No one is perfect and God did not make anyone to find a way to become perfect, so I am not insisting that any parent attempt to become some intellectual flawless trainer. You will struggle with bills, work, and at that life itself will deliver every possible complication it can your way. I am not implying you up and begin grabbing college applications to enroll yourself into school. While that is probably a great idea, I am implying that as parents and head of households, we at least consider reeducating ourselves for the chance at a better opportunity of educating our children. The mistakes you once made are not that unique that they are to never be made again. Mistakes will be made again and just because you suffered a great deal as a result of making those mistakes, does not and should never mean your child needs to endure the same course leading to that mistake being made. Remember that your child is in great need of guidance, and more importantly in even greater need of knowing what you are guiding them for.

Libraries are not just for students, they are open to the general public to guarantee anyone who needs information, will have it at bay. They are placing information either online or in books and I am sure my elders can verify T.V. tells you nothing, and entertainment, which distracts us from ever wanting to go to a library, will tell us exactly how to veer from such resources. A variety of Internet websites are consciously posted to take attention away from educational gateways, and thus redirecting not only the attention of adults but also their children into media controlled entertainment programs.

The effort to learn is obstructed by so much bilge, and when you give light to these obstructions you are avoiding what can be beneficial to not just you but your child's developmental capabilities. Gallons of information are yearning to be poured into a brain strong enough to neglect the programs designed, to keep the idea of organization and cooperation from ever being seen as possible. Hence the fact, we still follow rules developed centuries ago that none of us today have an opinion in altering.

Work is an every day obstacle, which physically takes energy away from getting up and going to the information daily, after you have just applied eight to twelve hours of labor into your day. Bills are mental obstacles we take on every second they are not paid off. The idea of work is forcefully converted into a positive act of survival, due to bills negatively existing as a hurdle on the course of surviving. By the time you actually reach a computer, you are practically dying for sleep or relaxing entertainment to relieve you from all the sedulous efforts to overcome your daily obstacles. As parents, the goal is to become educated but also generate a river of knowledge that our children – whenever thirsty – and only thirsty due to us informing them of what the thirst is, can use to become more educated with the programs of life and how to manipulate their choices, make a choice, and find doors to open with confidence in the results of what's behind.

Ever notice how a middle class working adult has organized a manageable schedule involving work, their children, and if any free time – free time. Seriously, how many of you today are in debt and still working with your children to schedule library visits at least once a week. Some of you are over the age of twenty-five and still are not intellectually adults. Why? This is due to being blind to valuable information that over years you have forgotten to learn after your mistakes were made.

While you are at work or home, your children are out teaching themselves but not necessarily learning the information that is of any intellectual benefit. Now, your children will not stop and they will continue to feed their brains chunks of information, from which they choose to learn. Weird enough – this starts at the age of three years old on a level where they can verbally display it.

Yes, at just three years old growing young and expanding your children are feeding their own brains. Mind you this is such typical information, however it is no secret anything typical our species willingly ignores. At just three years old, these little people are already asking questions and seeking the answers through response or research. Toddlers are choosing what they want to learn and I say choosing because even an infant has reasoning skills in development. Now, I mean no insult to your doctors and average psychiatrist who most definitely are fluent in their practice. At early ages our children are deciding what they will learn if we do not step up and conduct the patterns of their self-research. It is the reason toddlers ask questions over and over, and even the same question, which you may have answered twenty five times. I have a nephew, who is the brightest little young man, and he is only five soon to be six, and at two years old he began asking questions. One day at home he asked me, "Can I have a juice," and I asked him did he clean up his small action toys from off the floor in his room. He responded, "Can I have a honey bun." My nephew completely avoided question one, and as he did I replied, "No," he walked off and continued up stairs. Minutes later he came back down and asked me for a juice again. Now, I am no tyrant nanny to the kids, but I mean I cannot keep the answer negative, and then I thought to myself. I replied to my nephew, "Yes," and then he ran to get a juice comes back, I asked, "You do not want a honey bun?" my nephew said, "No." I then asked, "Be honest, did you want a honey bun in the first place?" He said, "No." I followed him upstairs and to my eyes surprise, I see all of his action figure toys are cleaned up and placed where they belong.

If you caught this like I did, my nephew asked me for a juice. I, then asked about him cleaning up his toys and he knew then he would not get a juice if his toys were not put away – knowing this, he asked for a honey bun knowing if I said no to a juice, I would say no to a honey bun. He then ran up stairs, which in fact after he asked for the honey bun avoiding my question knowing I would say no, and bought some time to go clean things up. He reasoned out the why and why not's of the situation and manipulated the situation to his view of it. My nephew's reasoning skills were at display and when I asked him if he knew what he was doing after seeing the toys fixed he just giggled.

Kids are not birthed into the world as growing infants and numb to learning until a certain age has been reached. The first thing children can learn they are going to learn, and as time progresses they eventually grow to the age where the need to know factor meets the need to find out: at an intersection.

The responsibility to educate your kids is now, and has always been, yours. Children will continue to reason out what they want to learn from school until they are out of school, and what they do next resulting in one of the biggest mistakes – many children across America are making, is try to survive through life with what they have chosen to learn in school after school. I am not asking you to do the teacher's jobs but your job and help develop your child's mind. What I am asking you to do is to make sure when the teacher's are doing

their job it is for a reason, and that reason will be
evident because their students will be consciously
deciding to learn beneficial information. This
information is direction that will guide students into
understanding how to analyze information, and from
there learn how to consider it as useful or non-useful to
establish a learning foundation.

Consider the affect a student deciding to not
learn has on the living systems of the world. Teachers
who are confident in their jobs and teaching techniques
have to undergo the realization of what they cannot
understand. Children choosing to learn information
other than what the teacher is teaching can cause the
teacher to feel as though they are not effective in their
teachings. This occurrence will mentally deprive them of
their skill and how well they will constructively use it. A
teacher that falls under the belief that they cannot
reach out to a student is dangerous. It affects other
students in the class when that teacher gives up on
their skill, due to the one or more students giving
attention to non-classroom activities.

Your children are yours for a reason because
they listen to you, and they try with the best of their
comprehension to understand you. When you display
methods of teaching they will display that they are
learning. Find time to learn to educate your children,
for the productivity rate of their behavior is dependent
upon your efforts. If you can reinstall information you
receive to your children, you also can witness how they
piece together what sections of your teaching they find
productive. However, when you do gain information do
not attain it with the thought in mind of what you want
your child to be. Gain the information with the goal of
ensuring that your child will have enough information
to guarantee more than one opportunity in their lives.
The prime goal is to give our children doors, several
doors, and if they want something reason the process
out and let them decide on what door of opportunity
they will essentially go through.

Read with them until they are reading to themselves. And, even then continue to read along their side surveying their performance until they need your assistance. Write with them and about topics you choose of the appropriate nature. Learn how to proof read written documents as well as how to interpret them. Create the time to build a mental library inside your own mind, where information is waiting to be transferred to your child.

Internet and Television are media resources leading as the primary interruptions in the course of parenting. Media resources are distractions that will keep you and your children from picking up a book, and also prevent you all from figuring out how to write your own sitcom someday, develop your own website, and/or create your own business. Take your children to the mall right after the library or alternate between various intriguing stores. Upon choice, allow clothes and shoes or gifts and gadgets to become the rewards for learning. During this time, out of the week take two days at least for two hours and go to the library. Your goal is create a learning schedule that cycle's information daily.

Most libraries are not over crowded, I said most; the reason for my caution in speech is because some libraries are far from being described as used frequently. By the ages of four and five take your children to the library and get them library cards. In due time, attempt to save up and purchase a computer, and then Google educational web sites and post books marks on them, or even leave them on your desktop for your child to discover.

Monitor the topic of your conversation around your children, but not limiting the topics to something only you feel that they can learn from. Parents are going to have their differences and are going to argue, but sometimes as adults we can argue and not realize the kids are around. By teaching yourself the proper facilities, you can still make your point without arguing. Arguing is difficult to prevent but it happens. At least, if the arguments are without control, make the awareness of information being used in arguments indiscernible.

As parents, we have control over how we think and allow ourselves to think. You can and should create the understanding and realization of the mind state fruitful to conducting the pattern of how you think. Consider the information you know now and ask yourself:

"How can the information I own, what I know now, benefit my child?"

Consider these thoughtful insights to develop an understanding of how your child should be educated. Being a parent is not at all easy for anyone, and the difficulties of being a parent will grow as the age of your child does. We are always going to be what we make ourselves, and even that takes time to blossom into our private reality. It takes time to be a parent; it is not something that adults or teens are just born to be. The responsibility of being a parent to a child last longer than just eighteen years of age. It takes so long to care for our children because we are not only trying to raise children to adults, we are also trying to raise adults into being parents. A transformation process from one mind state to another takes time and information, and information that you as a parent now will learn and distribute.

Listen, we have no idea, as of today, what our youth are getting into when we send them out into the world. Keep that in mind, as the youth venture through periods of experimental events and moments that as parents will nearly never see. Life progresses on and on and what you think you can assume about the life and our youth is not at all assumable to say the least. From our teens interacting in acts of internet porn, stripping out of their clothes on social sites, and combining the slang and foul language to say what one SAT word could define; the message is clear that we are going to be surprised at what they find a way to get into in the near future. We will continue to tell our children we been there and done that, nevertheless we have to understand what we have been through and done has advanced and will continue advancing as technology unfastens new public utilities. Try to understand what we think we know may not always be the best insight to what appears relative. Information comes to us at any age and is accessible at any time. Something you would not expect children to experience until the age of sixteen they will more than likely experience before the age of thirteen. Do the math on your own because the clock will not stop and neither will life's inevitable obstacles.

Position your parenting skills into an advanced psychological view, thus creating the plan of parenting to fill your child with knowledge. Help students learn how to get to school, and utilize what they already know as a result of your parenting, to have the will power to choose to learn not only what the teacher provides but what information is valuable in assisting them progress positively throughout life.

If our children are not learning from us, then they are choosing to learn on their own. When our youth get the wrong information in their minds, they will capitalize on the wrong resources necessary to apply the faulty information. I am almost accurate that by now you have noticed my repetitiveness in this chapter. I will continue to be repetitive because I know how frequent it is we see something new, and within hours, days, or weeks it is fairly old to us. This is a point of view we cannot allow to escape our attention span. Keep in thought that our children need us more than ever in 2013.

Misunderstood

"Along this life of growth there needs to be change. In order to succeed in that change, one has to understand Loyalty. Being loyal to who you are and accepting who you want to become will transpire in that change, only to lead a life full of growth and maturity."

-India Waugh

Individually, I am mentally and yet simply a claim of intelligence, but my relevance to an actual genius has a little indifference. Following what mentally leads me into a decision based off my intentional interest, by intentional I mean forced interest, I choose what weighs more or less positively or negatively – depending on the advantages and disadvantages of the current situation, circumstance, or task. Check the system, the way we operate is functionally unstable to others, from an outside view looking in. Everyone will take a peak and even some will stare at the obviousness of our character make-up, but never judging us by content only image reciprocation.

Misunderstood continued

Above is the brainless complexion of life we only accept when it appears one interchanging way. Change will never have an affect on the living origins of our broken societies, as the system of our society is indefinitely hindering the idea itself. The corruption in the system has long extended past simple follow the leader patterns. More insulting to our intelligence, we are incorporated in the formation of follow the follower. We are personally disrupted mentally and un-imaginably baring mind weights collapsing over our will to simply acknowledge anything. It is as if we act like fools with answers, and neither accurate nor acceptable are these answers, but merely a relative reference, which is portioned in distributed information amongst us. Unreliable thoughts are our processors, sending us into a reality made by explainable yet higher sources of un-debatable reason.

We have designed our own acts self-destructing capability. Re-enforced with what we ourselves cannot explain, we are accepted in the general public by our lack of supporting logic. My observation has allowed me to re-distribute the information we send out. A vivid observation reveals we are mentally confused by our incapability to accept understandings that exist based off evidence in actuality.

One person gaining the idea to explore what they intend to explain will be criticized and judged by the surrounding crowd. This particular crowd of individuals who find their reasons to explain anything, more reasonable than the individual stated above, and their reason, are those whose theory is alleviated by their self-supporting justifications taught by society.

I have seen too many people become thought eradicated, and the idea of common sense is a crime as the result of this type of eradication. Focusing on one single thought, one will guarantee they know, in confidence, because they have strong multiple perceptions on specific relative topics correlating to that particular thought. We all know it all when we believe we have seen, felt, and said it all, and no I do not myself have all the answers, but there are plenty of times where I feel like I know it all: now you can blame human nature.

Never would I have imagined we would mentally corrupt ourselves under the regulations set only to convince us there is order. I always assumed it would be a group over throwing theory by long shot fantasies. Not at all, we are mentally killing ourselves on our own accord due to lack of understanding the misunderstood. A body of useless information will appear useless if it is misunderstood. Or, maybe it is just me but the idea of one or even a group of people considering an object, subject, idea, or way of acting and determining our value in each is awkward and unreasoning. Clearly, only those who understand it understand the misunderstanding, or perhaps, they have willingly accepted that it is not understood; therefore giving them the impression it is okay to misunderstand it, and that is their understanding.

Ever make a word up or a funny phrase and some mind slave tool insist it is not a word or phrase.

How could they be right? What would be the leading resource in their argument?

Due to the fact your innovative word or phrase cannot be found where a group of people have decided the only active real words with definitions can be located, no one will justify the reality of your creativity. And, it is sad we cannot understand what kind of freedom we have because of the restrictions in place preventing us from being universally creative. In today's time, what freedom do we lack most?

Lack is a word that supports misunderstood topics, ideas, and personalities that are capable of actually being heard, interpreted, and reproduced. For a moment, do you mind if I borrow the phrase "Brain dead"? Brain dead is a state of mind I consider the loss of balancing one's own understanding and one's reason to understand. Many will read throughout this chapter and assume I am losing it or have lost the complete truth behind the functions of living. Truth is, we all have lost the pure perception of living, and we cannot figure out its configuration or the actual information that is pertaining to living to survive. Debatable at most, I will still beg to differ from what is considered logic and understood as man discovered and explainable.

I find it unarguably debatable that the way we dress and the way we wear our clothes is the idea of a group of people from the past, who figured selfishly their agreeing on any specific idea, is and always will be right. It is the faults of our own evolution over so many years to conduct our behavior under ways, which not from the bible – taught or learned, of man established reasoning integrated into the rules of society.

What are we functioning for?

It as if the world is spinning to be organized under the restrictions of one's ideal opinion of living, leaving us in other words, controlled. Take into consideration the attire you are responsibly required to

CC

wear in the event of a job interview. The requirement is the clothing that is labeled "Formal." A suit, slacks, and button up shirt that requires non-visible buttons are known as formal attire. I am curious, had the rules been set in tradition far back when, and the idea of formal had been baggy clothes and snapbacks, what judgmental era would society endure today?

MISUNDERSTOOD

Today, we lead ourselves by following the march making our next step congruent to the stepper in front of us. Funny how we attempt to embrace individuality through the information we only learn through following someone, a thing, or schedule. This is a confusing concept when the idea is that those who follow others pose no form of individuality. Some windows of vision are confined, and we must see deeper in order to advance the level of comprehension. As individuals we will grow our mind into successful graduates at overcoming our trials and tribulations.

"Today we prepare..." – Genesis Cole

Acknowledge the reality of who you are beyond the idea of what you want to be. Nothing is worse than being something you are not and believing you are that very idea. We have dreams and these dreams may be bigger than scales can measure, but without the truth we are subject to failure no matter how much we dwell on them. The belief of what you can be is completely different from believing what you currently are. Many of us like to call it acting. For most, the term is "faking" or false actions, speech, or way of thinking.

Lying about something you have said and performing actions that you have no knowledge of, will make your image seem more dominant psychologically. Due to this we are leading the blind with hopes to see the steps they can take into the future. When you imitate the reality of feelings involved in a situation irrelevant to your life, people who correlate to your replicated feelings are being misled into the idea of a bond.

The one fact that will shock us all, and even those who claim they are so "REAL" is all of us have our moments of imitation and are not capable of determining when or how. That is scary, it is one thing to be something you are not, but to be something you are not and then think you are not being that at all is subconsciously perilous. To aggravate life more, you do not even know what you are doing to not be that, which you are. Weird I must say, but while very confusing to witness, it is also necessary to study the fallacies of a propitious mind.

Have you ever told someone they were loud and not even seconds before you finished pronouncing the last syllable in the word loud, they jump to defense and ferociously ask, "What do you mean I am loud? How am I loud?" They act like what you are telling them has not been obviously observed and deemed evidentially true. People will fight the accusations until they feel no affect of the claim made against them. This does not help those who live in denial; instead it brings them surrounding judgment that they defy insensitively.

Pretending is the habit we all have passed along from person to person like a common cold. Right away, I already know many of you have begun denying the act, and even the possibility. Well my readers, can we just accept one thing, that being the possibility of you portraying the act of pretending.

Understand, that as humans we make mistakes and these mistakes – while sometimes often repetitive, are also unseen. In my opinion, I would suggest that at least 65% to 75% of our actions, which directly reflect our personality, go unrecognized. It is without doubt most difficult for anyone to actually look into the mirror and not see their best qualities, being as though that is all we can actually care to use the mirror for. So for those who find it hard to, try to accept what is possible beyond your own recognition.

Over and over the actions of our intriguing characters portray images, which we fail to identify with fortitude. The mind is lonely and seeing only what can be taken in and not brought out, due to our built in instincts to defend our own existence socially, physically, and psychologically. Our personalities are transporters delivering to others what they can accept about us. The window to our unhappiness is always cracked well enough to feel a breeze of change blow through. Nearly all of our capabilities – believed as such – inside our personality are misunderstood qualities.

The challenge of being misunderstood cripples us to the core, due to our incapability to acknowledge the surrounding characteristics that make us completely defined by our actions. This challenge is very significant and our concerns have value here, and the reason many of us are living these do as I've seen lives are due to the lack of value in our concerns. We can no longer keep our thoughts surrounded by the unruly leadership, organizing the areas of misunderstanding how we can become understood in a world that doesn't help you create yourself.

Various misunderstandings we suffer from are in the process of understanding our own personalities are what we need to observe with a close eye and ear. Establishing your opinions in thought but disregarding the act of placing how you feel into the reality of creating who you can be, contradicts your concern to advance in life. By observing what is being observed for you to witness, how we live without knowing who we are, will guarantee you seek to be educated in accordance to what position in life you intend to assume.

Factor in that you are capable, in many ways, of using the misunderstandings in society as resources to build your mind, your choices, your skills, and your true identity. Skeptical emotions towards laws and regulations are your signs of initiating a feeling of need to know, and fusing that feeling with information scattered throughout the programs formulated in society is a process of character redevelopment. You have conclusions to issues you have not brought upon yourself because of logicality. Human instincts can play into our favor as soon as we acquire the understanding that planned incidents are not always typical occurrences. Speculation is a tool more than it is a stem from anxiety. To wonder with interest but not limiting to positive or negative interest is beneficial, in the sense you feel a deeper side to any misunderstanding.

Learning to achieve the state of understanding you will take human instincts and logicality in addition to the areas of life we frequently misunderstand. Observation of such will reveal in the near future the actuality in reality, thus permitting you the use of mental and physical tools to distinguish personal development.

"I wake up every day with that make a difference attitude." – Genesis Cole

The Outside

"Everybody sees how you seem, however, only some know who you are."
- Ceazzar Corleone

You will never see my point of view coming from a distance, and even still my reference to my position on our challenges in life is as close as an eyelash. I am not referring to my actual position in the physical but more so the connection made in my mind, which I place in a conversation, verbal reaction to a statement, my answer to a question, and elaborating on the suggestions made by haphazard parties. In the mind, the messages we receive when reacting to life are far from what we anticipate to hear, when in close proximity of situations to see a shell of persuasion cracked and open. That shell may be known as the appearance of any noun. Witnessing the ideas of a perpetual thinker become physically brought to reality is probably the uniqueness involved with the capability to learn.

We see multiple examples of expression and well obvious gestures of depression-exposed daily as a reaction to life's trials. The core of who we are is where we assume the strength, put into any reaction, may be pushing out all the feelings or ideas to admit us into the state of emotional. This may become a rocky ride to endure this chapter but by all means bear with me.

It strikes us as almost the perfect acting theory to attempt to read a person and see all they can deliver unwillingly through their actions. This is because the will to actually control what you send out i.e. information, belongs to the mind. And, with no offense to any psychics, the mind cannot be read. Thinking daily of techniques to take your day higher than the last, you for some reason slow things down as you act far faster than you can think. That is chapter one people; review it before you screw it up.

Exterior disclosure of how we feel is almost impossible to keep under control. After all, we have the ability to react and reactions are kind of 50/50 on the good or bad scale. Feelings can come from one form of reaction some describe as instincts and from another

CC

form some label as "Stupidity". Which inspires me to arise the question, how is the decision that didn't go your way concluded to be the "wrong" decision, or thus the stupid one?

We'll get back to that in just a second, but for now I want you to focus your attention to something in the room you are in, other than my book. Take about five seconds to peak around, and I said peak not look – see you are getting distracted. Hey, look back down here. It will be there later. Now what did you see and as you think of the first thing you are probably asking yourself why. Why is what you are thinking of the first thing you said you seen? Was it due to the fact it was the first thing you saw, or possibly when you turned around it was the most significant item to stand out.
The connection you just made is connecting the interest in personality to interest in variation. Some things we will choose depending on its placement or where it is located. Of the crowd who turned around and the first thing they said they saw was the most significant item, placement is an issue to you. Think not, we'll see.

Those who responded to the first thing they saw, placement is not of high concern to you. And, if it were, without turning back around you would be able to say right away where you saw the first item you identified.

Placement is an issue of concern that introduces us into the high concepts of approach and acceptance. We rely on placement to make decisions more than we will ever believe. With nearly everything that has a choice, choice requires decision and decision is convinced by placement. The interest determined by like or dislike is argued by those with higher learning, and no offense, those select individuals will oppose the reality of evolution amongst human activity. We study human behavior looking for a reason to explain every single action, using every one by one step, we will every day to month to year learn about ourselves. Throughout this process of learning we are creating new patterns of activity i.e. habits and tendencies.

Speaking differently, acting out of typicality, and reorganizing thoughts are how we support the new understanding we have learned about ourselves. Placement plays its role as a learning tool to accept what is an interest discovered within, which needs to be brought out. Examples will vary when describing the use of placement, alternatively in thought; the fact stands placement is necessary to help what is learned outside inspire the discovery of whom you are on the inside. There are two sections of our personality, one is what we reflect on the outside and the second is what we hold dear on the inside. In most cases, we can acknowledge these sections by how we see something and how we feel about it. Certain situations you will act without thinking but only on the inside do you reflect differently those actions in previously experienced or imagined circumstances.

Envision a time where on the inside you felt a particular way about something you have never thought about but have acted on. That was the point where your feelings reflected the unsupported previous actions, just to acknowledge how you determine what emotions are placed in synchronization with your interest in activity.

Life has its own placement test for you. These test are the moments you decide style and taste based upon where you make your intriguing discovery. Various moments can be placement test when you find yourself deciding what fits. Placement is allowing what can go in your life to fit in and live with how it fits regardless if it is old or new reasons, but still accepting the fact whatever goes in has its use in your life. We bargain the issue placement with what and how we can take advantage of any noun or idea. For instance, take your clothes for example, you find a style that you like

CC

and you wear that style trying to impress not only others but yourself. The possibility of you finding that style old is high when you find your eye catching new style, which you find even more impressive. What do we typically do? We will switch styles and immediately find the new look reasonable because of its advantage on improving how we look.

So where do we get lost in this process of placement, it is when we switch from the old style to the new style and forget that the old style, regardless of how old, still kept you looking just as good. Placement is involved in the outside view of our personality and as we juggle with these interests we are leaving it outside of our minds. The two sections in personality are correlated to the determination of how we feel in response to what we believe is right or wrong. Due to placement, we have the capability to become fluent in distinctively analyzing what we do versus what we feel, in order to develop who we are. The process of understanding who you are is coordinated by areas in life we misunderstand. The challenge is becoming understood in a society that only prepares you to misunderstand yourself. Orchestrating your actions and emotions leads to you beginning the process of character re-engineering, and applying attention to your desires builds your awareness of how misunderstood you actually are.

Our lives are in the positions we place them in, and they will always indefinitely remain in those positions, which we leave them. When we are willing to see further into our lives as more than just what we desire but also what can help us and universally set us forward, doors will open and tables will turn. Periods of confusion have only existed through our lack of attention to what may not interest us through visual sight, but benefit us solely through its purpose and use emotionally.

I find the way to become more productive is to place the act of production into the process of becoming aware of misunderstandings placed around us. To deliver the unwanted interest into the wanted interest is undeniably advantageous. Resisting the will to think outside and act inside is possibly the reason for our misfortunate confusion misdirecting us in the search of truly understanding what God has designed us to become. We will always misunderstand who we are until we understand how what is misunderstood around us affects what is misunderstood about us.

Think about it.

Location

As relevant as this may appear to placement issues, which I described in the chapter — Outside. Location is a big mental challenge for all of us based upon the way we locate and re-locate our thoughts.

Have you ever begun to get into bed, turn the lights off, and get all tucked in and then you realize you forgot to use the bathroom? After you enter the bathroom and use it, you flush only to realize another thought has come to mind, or, while you still prepare for bed you no longer are getting into bed at that moment, but find something to do just before you lay down. Then you begin to wonder...

Well, why didn't I do all of those things before I got into bed?

If you allow me to voice my opinion solely based off what I have observed, and this is strictly pertaining to actions you have revealed unto me; our thoughts, ideas, and memories are poorly and unwisely re-located. The location of our priorities in thought are so tangled up that they are located in places where we cannot find them. Think about it, when you misplace an item you begin to question your sub-conscious and are now asking it to remember where in your mind have you stored the thought containing the location of the item, idea, or memory. You notice right away you cannot find the location as soon as you consider the thought of searching for it. In light of this discovery, you might find this statement familiar.

"My mind must have been somewhere else."

Reality is it is not your mind but the location of your thoughts that has caused you to feel displaced. We poorly locate our thoughts pertaining to various important subject factors in life because we position our thoughts in locations unfamiliar to our chain of connecting thoughts, which would allow us to find the answer or memory and even the idea, faster. For instance, take the way we organize our dreams and obligations as we begin a daydream.

A simple solution is smiling, because it is so temporary when we find ourselves struggling. We must still desire to smile in the midst of struggle to motivate our mind to conspire a way out of it. Smile when concerned with your late payments and uncertainty if payments can even be made. While you are devoting so much attention to not smiling, you are losing another mile on the drive to the location of the information – pertaining to the proper compulsory method of overseeing your obligations. Do not cripple your mood so viscously that you are unable to recognize your constructive thoughts.

Let us be honest to make a point fairly understandable to those who want to pay attention. What is it that we all desire: a car, a house, or several living necessities and so on. With the tree of needy wants will come branches of capable accessibility, and along these branches are leaves resembling significant understandings that either fall or withstand the winds of reality. Amongst other wants or needs we can add insurance – health or vehicle, and rent. You know you need a car but what do you do besides knowing you need a car, you also get picky. At this point you say I want this specific color, interior accommodations, auto this and that as well as any other technological advances.

Houses are very high in demand, and not to mention we all want the it would take two days to get to the other side of you home, house. Now comes the factors that do not matter but since God has allowed us to have fashion and taste – these factors exist. You have high priced clothes, tennis shoes, cell phones, televisions, handbags, and various materials we cannot take with us when we die.

Take all of the above and consider how your attention is pin pointed exactly on the target objective of getting these desires. Okay, now next let us allow some truth to become common sense.

With all these factors to consider, we need what medium or metaphorical bridge? MONEY. Here is where we misfile our thoughts so severely I am surprised any of us have not taken the mental placement test. We need and want these factors prior to thinking heavily on them constantly. In effort to acquiring such factors, every possible solution thought to gain them is injudiciously carved into the mind.

Our first discernible idea is to start out working anywhere we can be tendered a decent income. As you start assembling finances here and there, you have implemented a savings agenda. Natural is the thought of wanting to work a part-time or full-time job for money, but then again not at all when you can pretty much make money from anywhere, which is not our natural thought because we are too concerned with wanting before locating the real source of desire. This misconception or confusion leaves you trying to work anywhere higher income is capable, and the irony is even in the times of struggle we're obligated to a sequence of struggling to sustain the pursuit of desires.

Many of us are working to get by due to rough times being brought upon us unexpectedly. Even as things are bad, we still will wish for this and wish for that. We want and reach for products and materials that we feel more importantly can make our life comfortable. If you have not put the pieces together then allow me to confirm that the source of your primary thoughts are unable to be located where they can be understood. In other words, you do not know the true motive behind your desires because you cannot locate the thoughts connecting directly to your characteristics, which can define why you want and need what resource.

The mental challenge that we are distressed with is allowing ourselves to locate our thoughts in the respective order to our pre-designed patterns of life. I am not talking about God's plan; I am referring to the programs that only permit us to live in categories instead of created identities. We all can sit and argue the process and the complication that can arise from trying to locate your thoughts, from where you want them to be and where they actually are. It is far easier than we think to investigate this confusion and cultivate a solution.

Consider the various times when we have money that has multiple locations, and after the division of what we expect to financially make, we are hoping and praying we have enough to get what we want. Most of you, the morning of the first day of your pay week, developed an interest in an object on your list of intent to purchase. You will calculate your funds and rearrange some numbers applying your wages to match your financial destinations. After financial organizing, you pray for the left over change to be enough to purchase something you want. Why?

The process of organizing your funds can be revised to create a pattern for successful financial living. Imagine if we planned for our bills like we planned to shop, but just as willingly. Imagine if you thought about locating the part of your mind where your fashion and style would be, and found a successful financial stability plan. You are probably trying to determine now if the way you handle your bills is exactly how you would handle your desires. I am sure some of you already have a process you are well involved in. Just hear me out.

The same way you wait for those brand new shoes or styles, you could be preparing the bills or financial priorities to equip yourself with. The location of our thoughts can keep us in the difficult position we are in far more unreasonably than our actions ever can. Thinking is such a complication when we are giving stress the upper hand to determine our thoughts. Giving stress this authority is why we pay our bills exhaling and feeling relief, but it is also possible we could pay our bills with a smile and jubilance.

Your brain has a GPS, and this system is composed of your concerns. When the idea of something you need, or something you want to do comes to mind you begin thinking about it persistently, and that is your GPS system functioning and your brain is the map where the act of thinking is the searching program. Now being as though your concern is the system itself, what the concern actually is – the reason, is the address.

How many of you have forgotten to pay your phone bill or any bill? Or, have you forgotten to pay a miscellaneous bill, which the money to pay it has already been spent on something else?

And, how many of you forget to put your shoes on in the morning?

Can you at least see where I am taking this point of view? The level of concern towards putting on your shoes everyday is a clockwise rotational cycle uninterrupted by any other thought. Common at the most, you will never forget to put shoes on your feet. There is a city in your brain containing all the thoughts we everyday are continuously recycling. Many would call this the long-term memory bank, but if you ask me, between long-term and short-term memory, the gaps are a tad bit too big.

Due to you understanding the motive supporting your concern to relive this process of putting your shoes on every day, it is evident the thought containing the motive is located in the part of your brain you will never forget. Same thing goes for consuming food through your day. Many of you may become so busy that you may not get a chance to eat, but you most definitely will never forget that you have to eat.

Your bills and fees are possibly so far from this city they are in another state in your mind. We have this interest issue that causes a lot of concern for others and myself. We will consistently misplace the location of our thoughts simply because we are not interested in where we locate them. Take it from me, I am only twenty-five and I can tell you at this age I doubt that bills are going to stop coming, and I doubt the people who love sending them are going to get fired.

We do have a GPS system in our minds and we also have the address to all locations of our thoughts, however, finding these thoughts is the complex procedure creating difficulty when attempting to respond to the world with common knowledge. The more we challenge ourselves with the misdirection of thinking on our obligations and issues, the situation gets worse. We live every day oblivious to thought misplacement, and the process of losing thoughts will alter the result of controlling them, but never will the process itself be altered if we neglect the issue. The location of a thought representing the concerns you express to yourself subconsciously have motives, and we are not taking it serious enough to locate the reason and the idea, and merge them to understand what works and what is just happening because we are unaware. The challenge goes as far as bills and financial situations, and can stretch to something as minor as you forgetting to find something you misplaced. This is difficult and this challenge will become more difficult unless we practice how to align our thoughts into a pattern recognizable by will.

The solution to this challenge is not for me to provide, I have not the slightest clue to the process any one person undergoes, and neither do I have an idea to begin an assumption that one solution works for all. I can only provide what I see and what I hear, and conclude the challenge behind it all. Using our minds at will is more a challenge then we think, and living with the obstacles we already have obviously isn't keeping us in the position to focus more on controlling where information is placed and why.

I made a decision to locate my responsibilities – financial and as a father – in the same city in my brain that putting on my shoes is located. Make the priorities and the solution to your priorities repetitive, but also allow yourself to be able to identify how one relative coalesce of thoughts creates understanding and definition in the locations of another. Even if the solutions are temporary, the practice of thought positioning and locating will cause growth in actions correlating to ideas.

Ask yourself, what do I need to locate in my city of thoughts, which will help me establish consistent and constant reoccurring solutions to modern indefinite issues?

NOTES:

Patience

"All tables turn, it doesn't matter which side you are sitting on."
- Ceazza Corleone

It strikes me so painfully as if I were shot at close range by a thirty-eight revolver and survived, but only to absorb the pain rattling my nerves as I wonder if I will persist to live with my injury. Every day, waking up is unbelievably senseless if you are aware of the inconsistent acts of relaxation. With no succession, to open your eyes and witness a day you know and can predict very well, it seems like you only feel your pupils breach your eyelids to read the same book every year and every month, with the same chapters. Every week, you will review the same topic and reflect on the same pages. At some point, you will ask yourself when does the struggle to live end?

I feel like I wake up morning after morning knowing what I can do, what I have to do, and what I am willing to do, but even considering the ideas I feel no subtle approach to acknowledging the strength to be expressed, when living out these understandings. We all wake up some mornings or evenings with the questions starting with what. What if you could instantly change your career? What if you could instantly become the evidence of your dreamt life achievements?

The questions will become more questions, and as they do, we will answer them with our mental ears. Leading our beliefs never against our questions as answers but as blank messages, and then hearing the thought of change and responding to it appears today preposterously uncommon. The big question; alternatively when we have these thoughts of changes – how often are we acting out the changes in our minds?

Even if the change is in your capability deemed as impossible, the possible is only what we attempt in our effort to show because we believe it is in fact possible. In many cases, we are going to stare at the trials and tribulations of life and fuse together our thoughts, only to come out with an overly imperfect plan. It says a lot to look at what you don't want to do and think about what you wish you could do, while debating why you cannot let either co-exist in your decision of compromising with them both.

I began my career in writing reflecting on what wasn't given to me and what doors were never opened for me, the pain of being the center of an insult, and at times the bulk of popularity.

With the frustration of making a better way from a life that looks like there is never a better way or any way, you can become more in life through your efforts – and using your efforts to bring all the can's and can not's into a created inevitable collision. As a result of this collision, give yourself the decision to use this consolidation as you desire.

The road that leads you to success is always abandoned and deserted. Why? Due to the fact you are not suppose to take that road, because taking that road means you have abandoned the original predesigned program, put in place to keep your life controlled. You are not permitted to know what is at the end of the road to success, because knowledge of such rewards is deleterious to organized programs if shared.

Greatness has its struggles, and on the road to becoming someone great the struggles are designed to come at you hard. Once you decide to turn onto this road, those in charge of your program will see you and want you to immediately stop forward progress, and turn around or deviate. The objective is to ensure you turn back to your regularly scheduled program and continue to ride with the false impressions of a worthy destination.

Evidentially, you work and struggle to take care of a family, not just financially but as well mentally. The bills and payments program coordinators know you care dearly about – because your income can barely be kept stable, have to maintain some idea of future relief.

To elaborate, on the road (program) you ride to sustain the idea of living is an outcome that has been planned for you many times over, and many years before you were born. Keep in mind this planned outcome is not the outcome God has designed for you.

As you are on the road you are on now and are coming up to the corner where you can turn onto the road to greatness, every time you do not turn the plan that is prepared for you by God, changes, and the program does not have to adjust to you not turning because obviously they still control your destination. Okay, so with that concept in mind now the bigger and better concern is, why do you keep passing the turn to greatness?

The road you are on, which is the program, is simply a huge circle. Re-lapping this road causes you to run a course that will strike to be smooth and faster as well organized. Yes, the road is rough and has its bumps but respectively you have been circling it for so long, you have developed acceptance. Seeing the 'this is what I have to do' in every re-lap.

Ever tried something big and the event itself were significant to you, and the outcome was as great as you intended it to be. Many of us as teen students have tried various activities, such involving sports or music or personal development events. For females, there may have been cosmetology or singing, and for some even class presidents. Ideas can sound good, but as soon as you turn into that creative act of self-expression, and set out your efforts towards that expression, there is always this case of multiple situations that manifest in your life.

Situations either you have not experienced or ones you deal with daily, and few annually are brought to attention more seriously all due to you beginning your risky talent stretch. Such factors like criticism, financial responsibility, and educational consistency are all related concerns that come up when you begin this effort to express. Problems become jealous of your efforts and creative ambitions to express your talent, and furthermore desire your attention desperately. This is why we experience so much when we are on the road to greatness. Think about it...

What we need to acknowledge is the fact that once you turn onto the road to greatness, the problems were on the road are going to turn behind you and try to follow you. Regardless, the fact you are now on the road to greatness means you are in the lead, and if the problems follow you then the problems are behind you indefinitely. Why give problems you have put behind you the time of day to catch up and ride with you?

This is where our challenge begins with our presence on the road to greatness. The road to greatness is not a smooth ride, and the direction you embark on this path is not an organized and routine programmed schedule. You are going to jump in and out of various situations and explore more, but still endure new obstacles and test. The information you well knew has now become a real test of usability. The challenge is our patience.

Many of us believe faith takes us where most who only have confidence – will never go. The truth is faith will carry us along a road with so much confusion and provoking self-destructing moments, confidence is the strength in soul to control the wheel and keep straight. Faith is the essence of patience and also the undeniable cause to beginnings we thought we would never have.

Patience plays its role to help us learn as we go without clashing into every problem we come to, and as a result, stressing over the conflicts dramatically. Several of us get involved in different activities and occupations, and are forcing their belief in focus based off the results of the act alone. That is the pothole on the road to greatness and the stoplight that changes every season.

Patience is not pursuing greatness and having results in your piece of mind. That is not patience at all, that is pertinent to when we give anything expecting to get something back. You will never get back when your

CC

only effort giving in was premeditated. Blessings are brought to us through the genuinely observed actions and reactions. I analyzed our actions and have noticed many of us would never turn onto the road to greatness, because we lack the patience to, are not willing to suffer a short period of time to live blessed over a long period of time.

We could encounter countless blessings possibly for the rest of our living lives, and then again that exact reason itself is the reason many of us lack the patience to see these hopeful happenings through. After all, when it comes to what we feel we deserve, we hate waiting.

Take also into consideration; we lack patience even when we feel we may not deserve anything. When someone is insisting it upon us we then surround our opinion with their reason, and thus postponed rewards begin to be impatiently waited upon. The intention to receive becomes stronger and thought of receiving more connects to the fact we didn't want it before, because we did not know we deserved it. With any present reason, our impatience builds over the understanding of what perception we grab from desiring our wants and needs. This is the course that drives us to a point that we bargain our success with faster results. Many of us are going through the struggle and the problems life can bring, and are focused on the greater road. Even then, we still make the mistakes a lot of people who are great now have made. We swap small moments of pleasure for unwisely outcomes.

The moments are the individual places in struggle where you may want or feel you need a break through. Moments can be where instead of us consistently saving for a new house for our family, we want the new car and set out to attain it.

Where the break from stress is wanted, is the medium within your strive to reach success, and yet, while we see a break there is still more road to go on.

The outcome of lacking this reality is after all you have been through, all the bills and frustrations, and as well the consistent days of barely keeping ten dollars to your name, still sustaining an impatient demeanor.

We remain impatient with the only terms in life that can bring us the focus needed to inspire ourselves. Provided the reasons that we go through what we endure, there any many ways we can bring inspiration out of devastation. Once tragedy hits, we feel we need to maneuver and manipulate our way through the bad into the first good situation we come across. Most of the situations we put ourselves into involve circumstances that lead us on the same road, before we decide to turn onto the road to greatness. Impatience enforces the need to seek a way to just get by, but it does not permit us the ability to see a long-term solution to any life obstruction.

We allow our impatience to keep us out of focus and that focus becomes the key to keeping us out of faith. Once we are out of our faith, we feel as though decisions to get us out of a situation are to be made not only with the intent to get by, but seeking the expeditious advantage.

I have seen rainy days and I have been in uncomfortable positions in various situations, and the status of the situation keeping me so down and out in a stressful sanity, I began to develop a plan that will get me out and keep me out with the best advantage. It sounds good, it sounds like a plan but that is not our job. Your job is to keep your patience, keep your inspiration, and not lose your focus but keep your faith and watch God work.

CC

God is your advantage and God gives you not only the outlet of getting by, but the full proof exit. See we like to run with the solutions that permit us to move out of one level, but unfortunately do not help us migrate to the next. We want to make more of the conclusion and the only way to do that is to factor in faith in God, thus inspiring confidence as well wisdom to understand the movement from one situation to the next. You are stuck in debt buried to your neck, and feeling the stress from school and work is taking an intolerable toll on your soul. You will find your inspiration and see your way out eventually, but do not worry about advantage because God is your advantage and God is keeping the benefit waiting at the exit of your struggle. God only wants you to know you can pull through and God will do the pulling if you do the pushing. The effort to pull is the act of getting by – to continue pulling even outside of your struggle, is point in struggle where you see advantage. God does not and will not loosen his grip on the rope of progress, God has you tightly in his grasp and as long as we continue holding on, we will be pulled along the road to greatness with patience.

Patience can seem like it is necessary to be applied in the worst moments in your life. But, just think about those individuals who suffer from Dyslexia, imagine the patience they must endure to learn simple principles that come to us with little practice. There are individuals who must learn to use technology to their advantage in order to simply speak. Frustration can build fast as you live amongst others who do such a task with ease, while you struggle to complete with the process of moderate communication.

Relaxed demeanor and approach to obstacles can form a different person out of you, because you began to want what you are waiting for more, and also expecting it faster. The ideas will come a lot faster, and these aren't ideas of getting out, these are ideas to keep you away from what you are going through. Honestly, if gaining the control we desire over how we live was as easy as flipping a switch on the wall, how many of us would have learned from the events we encounter? Of course we wouldn't want any of the problems, which would result in us receiving no natural education at all. We would make every turn towards the exit of our original program and we will never see the problems we overcame to understand the problems we need to overcome. Due to impatience being such an incredibly cancerous like factor in our lives, let me ask you a question. Right now, develop the image of you in the lifestyle you would ask a genie for, or pray, wish, and keep your faith for. Now, with that position in thought – imagine you never went through any of the troubles you have experienced, all trials and tribulations were vanquished.

"Vamoose"

You are now in the position of your life you could probably label as greatness. Well, being as though you are in this position of greatness, think now back at everything you ever went through, everything that brought a little confusion to a mass outlet of stress and depression.

Would you rather be impatient and gain the blessings and rewards of service and live with what you think is the idea of comfortable, and go through what you never went through and all the pain while in the life of greatness?

Or, my readers, would you rather be patient, keep your inspiration, maintain your focus and allow your faith to grow so strong the struggle you are going through now, which has you feeling like nothing, converts to having your struggle end and stress thrown away as your anxiety is abolished to a minimum level of fear, and as a result – receive your blessings and rewards permitting you to live as comfortable as God promised?

Think wisely because it is not as good as it seems to get blessings without wisdom, especially when the great turns to good and the good falls to bad. Oh yes, it gets very ugly but there is nothing greater than to be patient and have God turn your bad into better, your good into greater, and you into a product of his glory. The road gets tough and the times get harder but with patience you create the opportunity of being blessed with relief and not character repression. We all will wonder what we can deem acceptable to go through in life, and with patience, you are going to find your way through faith that regardless of what you endure, you will establish a foundation of tolerance.

Patience can bring us out when we think we are too far in, or get us in when we are stranded out. Having patience is the processor of all beneficial balances to understanding what you felt through struggle is what you needed to feel, in order to help you determine how to witness how great you can become.

Be patient for the road that appears great is only the program showing limited results of surviving, and that road will never have the feeling of greatness as you ride along it. Once you reach the end of that road, you will find that there is nothing worthy of sustaining life comfortably. It is when you turn onto the road to greatness, you come to realize with patience comes the best rewards God has ever prepared for you.

Help

"The one who takes your hand but touches your heart is a true friend."
- Ceazzar Corleone

CC

The psychological situations of today strike me with more concern than any conflict brought along the path God hath me walk on. As stated before, riding along God's designated road is much more rewarding. Forgive me of my language, but the bullshit is building by the canyon. I mean it is as if people provide themselves to help but they cannot bare the room for mistakes to be made, neither ignore the anxious eager to indulge in one's self interest if the possibility of harm being done to them prevalently exist.

Clearly, as I state my position high in manner and respect, is it possible those who claim their pureness in humanity are surely the worst example of humane, which today indisputably our country needs.

Take my old position working as a part-time employee; I worked forty-five minutes away from home, which contradicts and challenges my need to seek a high interest in goal setting. I dared to be an author, as it seemed others double dared me to achieve that dream while partaking in retail. Knowing this reality, I also dared myself to find help. My decisions now or later – to pursue, I bickered back and forth with my self-conscious mind dubiously.

I am neither to complain nor make it my concern, the issues of my life I dislike but refuse to act on. God has me in favor and in mind just as I have my faith higher than stars in God's works. Babbling in the stockroom, I dreamt heavily of a career worth the suffering, and every thought reflected a book and ink pen frolicking in the comforts of my palm.

Unfortunately, people can no longer use the terms family or friends with me. Call it as best you feel or capably can describe it, but family or friends are words numb to me like an incision made beneath the lights hovering over a surgical team in the ER. They have no meaning and no cause.

Every exchange of action is business, the acts of what used to be courteous are now known as business. Everything is business, and nothing is favor or just cause, due to the reality no title and name can back up what is practically business. The world is run by money and money has brought so much fear upon our people, we are scared to help each other in fear of what we may lose.

We are blind by our own deception and eager will to receive money that we hound and hunger over to succeed, and if that is even the least of bad words used to describe the progress of this process. We seek financial benefit and set our goals with money in mind.
Where can you see generous genuine cooperation and courtesy?

Business has become the overall factor in healing techniques applied to the wounds of individuals who need help. When you need a lift from someone who posses a vehicle, you will also need gas money, which if observed logically is a business exchange. When you need somewhere to stay, or you request help with bills or rent, it is not favor it is business exchange. To help someone with lunch or providing any financial assistance in foods service is business.

Every action displaying the kindness used to be the example of unselfishness and caring, yet those acts have now been transformed into business. Our actions portrayed, are only actions of give and get back. That is business in the logical sense that is profitable tender and exchange. We all are struggling because we lack the effort to seek a motive or reason, or explanation that does not involve money.

Even if you have money, would you then help?
No, because you are scared if you help someone you will then be at a disadvantage because of it. Greed has overcome our living purposes, and because of that

we just want money now. Hence the programs false evidence appearing real. Why do we not want to see others climb and reach new heights of success with us? Ask yourself, why is success an individually sought idea?

Answer line:

Instead of team-orientated success seeking units, we rather struggle in our own self-built competition to rise against each other. Foolish is he that aims for individual success believing that the peak of it is more comforting, than knowing not only did you succeed but you brought four other successors with you. Misunderstood are the channels of life we tune into trying to accomplish any objective pertaining to our dominant survival, and I fear greatly labeling these objectives goals. As much as we bark and attempt to contain order over other countries, yet, I cannot see why another country has not tried to exchange similar savage acts amongst us.

Our America has brought the worst kind of struggle upon us. This struggle is the lack of support for each other. Designed programs have installed a monetary system controlling our resources. As body of people we cannot even support each other without the primary purpose of surviving causing us to clash selfishly in effort to acquire essential resources.

Why should anyone have to work harder than another to barely make an hour of what someone makes in minutes. We have ground our people into a mind state that seems all but the right words to describe out country. I live here and want to appreciate it, believe me. Unfortunately, this challenge is beyond treacherous. How hard the feeling must be to try to accept what lifestyle has been influenced and not by our own will discovered.

You cannot even have raw talent any more because every ideal gift is now made into a battle of expression. Check your local cable guides, search through your channels to see any example of this modern day gladiator lifestyle we have embraced. Everything is a competition and everything is a fight in some competitive effort to succeed.

That is what I am supposed to tell my son, that you have to fight to survive. I believe there is a very distinctive difference between fighting and working hard.

- America's got Talent
- ABDC
- We have turned poetry an emotional release system into a competition.
- Culinary arts is a competition and factors like natural intelligence, creativity, singing, musicians, lyrical master minds of composition are all degrading their talent one by one to express they have a talent period.
- Art and even interior decoration has now become a tool for finance.

Whatever you dream to do or become and desire to build your success with has been monopolized. Much if not all efforts to express pure talent has become evidential unnecessary obstacles. Program coordinators want you to hurt, be selfish, and be individually ignorant to the concern and where about of others. Life has become a race to survive and not an improving process by means of a country sharing knowledge and God giving benefits to survive.

Individuals I speak to everyday are saying, "Man you just have to get a better job, you just have to get out here and get this money." I have not had one conversation with anyone, and I mean not one person, and his or her point of beneficial growth in living is not or has been not self-financial based advancement. Not one person. No one is or has actually implied or referenced you to do what you want to do in life, solely because they know with the programs set in place it is nearly a law-breaking attitude to seek out that uncommon pattern of living.

No one at all will introduce this program deviating idea; everyone will only introduce the program. The same program which keeps us struggling and selfishly knocking each other down to survive. We do not motivate each other at all. We gloat and tare down the bridges of destination with our selfish inspired pursuits. As a matter of fact, it is our involvement – our devoted pledged membership to the program causing us to defeat each other. But wait, they say you have a choice and this is true – you do. Alternatively, without the motivation or the support to steer you in the direction of an educated lifestyle, your choice is useless.

Right now anyone can choose to be the President of the United States, but with how much lack of motivation do you think or know that person could still lack and make it.

I'll be back for that answer, for now I will give you some time to congregate on that idea.

We do not physically and mentally motivate each other nationally or universally. The fight is on, because the mind of many citizens today is I will succeed by all means and any selfish means, and if that includes fucking you over and over and over and over and over then I will do it.

You cannot attempt to be what you want to be in life because people are constantly de-motivating the act of seeking valuable information worldwide. Information – valuable information – is controlled and only distributed to those of select stature. However, this does not limit the ability to locate and discover this information being kept from you. But the rub is that you have to know you want to know it because you know you need it, and my fellow citizen, they are not going to tell you that you need information capable of relieving you from the laws of programs designed to keep you financially restrained.

The negativity is in the guidelines of the program, and the program has been set in place long before we can ever consult the motives supporting the existence of such programs in the first place. We are already large in numbers in our nation and this is excluding our government. Do not even bother to entice your curiosity of journeying their road to obsolete organized power. As human beings created to love and bond with each other, the change we seek our government to bring will and can only come through us. Will we change business back into favor, and change the process of give and get back benefits into the selfless idea of "just cause I want to help."

How far will we rather watch our own fall into pits of failure and poverty? Genders feud over this program, man and woman cannot get along cause of this program placing emphasis on the details of intercommunicating conflicts via media and entertainment. Children and teenagers are constantly motivated poorly because of the manipulated resources and hidden knowledge buried within the program. A lot of you may not like the truth, and I damn sure do not either – clearly because I am explaining it.

Interesting enough, I will leave you with this. I sat next to a stranger and brought this topic to moonlight, as they heard me out and reflected on the perspective of my observed reality, they replied, "That is life, that is America, and that is the way things are."

Really?

Offer up

Currently, it is obvious we need admissible reasons to become courteous. Acts of respectable kindness seize situations only after the internal perception, which brought out as an opinion, is a factor.

We breathe oxygen poisoned with give and take and take some more, take a lot, and finally taken too much. Yet, the sensible act of giving is merely portrayed as if a law. Much of what we do as a favor is recorded by those whom we have done favors for as an act of goodness, but the act itself makes us collude the intentions of one who does any favor.

People are not shit, a sad truth developed long ago but consistently living. The values of our determined actions are lacking altruistic visibility. Individually, we tare down the respectful rules of courtesy leaving it in rubble of untrustworthy incentives. Looking in the mirror, it is harder to understand why you are who you are when the reflection is even itself everything you want it to be. People continue to see themselves for what they want to be, tendering their characteristics like money. Anywhere character traits can be used they are, and this reckless usage causes people to see the individual side of life.

Giving is an action performed when a benefit seems dominant in ones favor. Unfortunately, before we confess to the act of giving with intent to benefit, we will deny that we do this. As we hold a conversation with others about lending and borrowing, it will lead to you speaking as if you'd give your last dollar away to anyone who needed it, but knowing good and well God has and will test us everyday with situations where giving more than we keep is a decision. But, we are too scared to help others as a result of a flaw in our individual mindset. Seeing someone down and out, you will become fearful that if you assist him or her, you will end up falling down because of your keen gesture. Where is the faith in having a realistic optimistic attitude?

A troubled thought in the mind, which is causing confusion, is proving we no longer think for the group benefit and outcome – because we individually seek success. Being scared to offer up your services by means of anxiety for your life's progress is only a concern when you fear your capability to survive. Ignorance is causing us to see what we will not do over of what we can do as an unhealthy decision. It becomes obvious if we have not already noticed; everything that we will not do is the act that if ever done, would make the most difference. The change this world needs is hidden in the actions we refuse to make for reasons society has installed into our instincts.

"Nearly everyone is walking the wrong way..." - Ray A. Coleman

Walking the wrong way is what we will do if we are not influenced to do otherwise. It is like we have been following detours and reading awful directions for the longest unprogressive period of time.

Our eyes will never see the beautiful composition of change due to the open effects of individual mental disclosure of un-resourceful instructions. Shutting down all channels of what generally causes likeable changes in our susceptible mind will simply become the lead by interest into casual fields of negativity. Responsibly, we must heed the fact we do not acknowledge the out and open enterprising information, which can further develop confidence in supporting others. The broad display of what can alternate wrong from right is masked behind acts we only see made in ignorance, but coordinated by higher powers. Even as a group, we can combine our individual interest into a major act of negligence, and in return we end up driving down the roadway to hell. People are chasing the same dreams for self-success and are all individually failing as a group. Is that not progressing backwards?

Seriously, we are really going to continue to watch each other struggle to be successful, and provide no support, which is honestly what we all need to provide together so that any goal is achieved. A helping hand has lost its definition. Excuses of an unbalanced reality cause us to use the phrase "Do you need a hand?" as a brownie point collector. Yeah, it sounds good but when the meaning of its spoken form actually needs its performance, we tire of the idea and shade the sight of our actions.

Realistically, be advised of the hidden truth, the truth you are forced to overlook or under value. We are scared to offer up our services because we as a people are challenged mentally with the perception that help comes solely from finance, that giving help will bring you self harm, and that uniting to set upon an objective is the inimical strategy.

Wake up people, money is a tool that has remarkably been converted into the spenders' prime idea of a necessity, and as well it has forced us into becoming the tool. Everyone is chasing a dollar because they believe a dollar makes a difference. The difference has never been material and it never will be when it boils down to surviving together. No matter what you give, favors or debt in any form of material, the biggest change in society will come from our actions acting together.

I am sure all of you have been asked by a friend or co-worker for a favor, and nine times out of ten it involved financial distribution on your part. What is our next response, we feel as if giving up money is a task too difficult to take on. Well, as understandable as many of you will make that particular perception appear, just what is your alternative way of giving besides finance?

You do not have an option do you, and possibly the reason you feel so burdened by giving out financially is because you do not think about what really makes the favor a favor, besides the involvement of money. Think about it, you bestow money for anything, and the receptor of your financial favor becomes jubilant and highly influenced with the idea they have been blessed. What do you think is going to happen next? They spend it. You give people money and it will get spent point blank. What did you change?

NOTHING.

Next time we consider the proposal of favor, and before we insist we are being so generous to haplessly find out our generosity is limited to insufficient progress, and attempt to discover what is the cause for financial failure.

Use your heads people. We are leaving everything up to money like the importance of it can keep a tractor-trailer speeding at 80mph from crushing you. No it cannot, take the fear of not having money and incorporate ideas of what favors can inspire to the foundation of a team. Your faith is shot beyond a dead battery because you have ignored any ulterior purpose to support any individual other than finance.

On the alternative side of giving out financially, money is residual. Either you will have it constantly or you will not and that fact is constant. Giving it away is a decision that we should accurately and thoroughly make. Many of us give away financially, and are doing so because we want to be nice but truly feel as though we were better off keeping our money.

I have given away my last to strangers, co-workers, my family, and the mother of my child. They never know it is my last but it is true I pass it on along without fear of being without. Before you look at me like I am clearly out of my mind, first understand my faith. Money comes from working, and to work is a blessing. As long as you work you get paid. God looks out for his people as we persist to genuinely look out for each other. By God's grace I have a job, by his blessing I keep my job and work to become greater than average as it is in accordance with God's will.

Really though, God has never let me down and every time I have handed out money, I have always remarkably seen it back through God's merciful promise in blessings. What we need to understand, mentally, is that receiving money back is not always the blessing. Read that last sentence over again, I know that may have been tough to swallow for some folk.

On multiple occasions, when I have given out money, money was not what I received back. Blessings come back according to the actual changing benefit significant on your obsequious quest. In other words, what really matters in actuality pertaining to how you will grow with wisdom, will be the recipient of colossal blessings from the spout of God's canteen. We are scared to give away our money because we want it back as soon as we acknowledge its swift absence.

Offer up what matters, change is going to come through our actions alone, but when you add in the favor of God, change transitions into an advanced experience. Someone who is in need of a job can use you taking them out to get apps, make phone calls, and assisting the set up of interviews is offering up your true services. I have seen people ask for gas money to go out and get applications for employment, and to that individual they believe help has actually been applied.

Come on now, it is crazy that we feel like we have really helped someone through financially aiding his or her misunderstanding of their own worries. It is more to be done in our society, which involves giving opportunity to others and doing so in various other areas of life. Money is not opportunity, however, it is the false identity of control and control is the biggest form of deception. To assume you have control you will furthermore assume you have power, and having power only influences the pleasures of man and not the wisdom of the word, which coincidently are over looked for the pursuit of treasury. It is an unfair opportunity for the receiver of money tendered in the act of favor to do something stupid, inevitably the result of ignorance. We as a body of people need opportunities in the form of doorways and windows, unveiling to you every resource that can be indubitably accessible.

If we are going to be snobby with our money, than we can at least wisely present favors that are most effective in progressing life – rather than momentarily enticing it. Provided the opportunity to become what any individual can conspire to evolve into, one needs illumination in mind. The confusion of money being an objective is the dropout resort opposing the fact many of us are ignorant to the actual definition of opportunity. How many people will act on what they do not know, only to discover a repetitious cycle of spending? We allow the blind ambition of a dollar to keep people individually moving but separately not progressing.

You can read this and turn your face however you want, but understand as every chapter will inform you, this is not my opinion. This is specifically what I have observed from the actions of multiple individuals online and in person. We are falling behind in progress because we misunderstand how to help any individual. One of the most ineffective contributing parts to helping anyone is picking and choosing who we desire to offer our services up to, as this bounds us to creating an endless pattern of isolation. I remind you, no matter whom you help everyone obtains the strong possibility to make mistakes time and time again. Why feel obliged to one person who can still spill milk just as much as the next person?

Seeking these individual obligations is embarrassing to the grind for success. We will continue to be challenged by the misunderstandings of ourselves, and then continue to misunderstand each other in the process, all while still ignorantly and selfishly trying to enrich life. The creation of a global climb for all can be established by our own will power to acknowledge what makes the difference made positively salutary.

You need to ask yourself some questions, one of them being why do you fear helping others, against all the evidence that reveals man will sin, and thus must be encouraged by the word and his brother and sister in Christ to know otherwise? Every chapter before this one is creating the understanding you will need to obtain in order to constructively renovate the inner you. As we began to develop a more profound relationship with God and the word, we are sub-consciously re-programmed and taken from societies desperate predominating views. You must understand how misunderstanding what it means to offer up – is a mental challenge.

Creating You

"We are growing older but we are not growing wiser." – Kelvin Fields

Finally, as I am looking down the road to success I see what appears to be the aftermath of the movie "The Day After Tomorrow." I have found the door to the slaughterhouse, the gates to disaster, and picturing the turns and exits I will have to pass up just to be more determined to reach the end of the road, and not just ride on it purblind.

Success is at the end of the road and we never see what the finish line looks like until we are done riding the road, adjusting to its turns and obstacles, and conflicting with lane swerving drivers. Bills are your informal green signs posted high where no matter how many times you pass by one, you will always see another. Living habits, styles, and tendencies are your lanes that we go in and out of trying to keep life from slowing us down. Exits are our mistakes and trials, which we sometimes take bringing us off of our road. Turns are just curves in your life pattern(s) progressing you into what appears as a difference in your day. We ride these roads speeding while some are looking for the Program directors that are well known as the interstate police. Various programs are in the path we choose to take and once we change paths that program director searches for you. Directors never want you to go to fast in life, and when you do they become offended to see you go fast especially with complete control.

Living from lane to lane, and jumping into others lives and having them switch lanes, will take them off of their directed course. Some make it back to that lane while most others do not.
What happens when someone jumps in front of you in your lane? What do most of us tend to react with?
We switch lanes and try to go around that person who has invaded your lane.
Next, we try to speed up in a lane that is not even ours, and then shoot pass anyone near that lane to get in

front of them and progress back into your lane. Lane switching takes about two to three seconds or possibly minutes, and consider those minutes to be metaphorically speaking relative to days, months, and years. When you jump out of your lane to get past someone that has invaded your lane and get back into your lane, you have just spent days or months probably years out of position from where you were supposed to remain. As well you have decided to take yourself from your lane and completely misplace yourself from events and situations that were designed for you in your lane. For a moment, it almost appears like you may have avoided some trouble up ahead, but are you sure that is trouble, and are you sure you want to avoid it?

As you spend this time out of your lane missing what was designed for you to go through in that lane, you are now in someone else's lane and as well putting yourself into a new program full of obstacles and trials that were not even meant for you. This is where we become mislead, trying to ride the road and letting every little distraction take us out of our lane. You can spend years in another lane trying to get back to your lane, while experiencing moments in your life other than what your lane has prepared for you. In life, we are on the path to success, yet we allow the smallest to biggest conflicts, and misunderstood situations, deviate us off that path.

Take for example, above I referenced bills being the big green boards informing you of the current or upcoming locations, and as well what lanes take you to reach those locations. By allowing someone who has entered your lane to jump in and push you out of your lane, you are now passing by these green boards and facing bills that are not designated for you. We create new complications of living with our decision to react to those who merge into our lanes, and attempt to send us down an unprogressive road.

It is practically always successful for others to create changes we cannot choose to make in our own lives. Powerfully thought and questioned, I wonder if we consider that when we witness someone swerve into our lane, why should our first instinct result in us deviating from out of the lane we are in? God has everything planned for us and as God works in mysterious ways, one method that should be obvious to us is God's desire to be there for us. People are going to jump in and out of your lane, slow you down in your lane, and others will press your bumper to rush you through life. Regardless, whoever swerves or cuts into your lane, your lane is your lane, and whoever they are; they are only in your lane for as long as God wants them to be. When the time comes for them to go they will leave and your lane will be clear again.

The confusion of understanding how to look at what the roads look like now and anticipate what it can appear to be later is prevailing. The confusion will be there and stay as long as you try to move along the road without concentration on your objective. Clearly, stopping on your road is a death option, so alternatively, why switch lanes, which can alter what path you are taking and the destination of it. Let's be more considerable to the circumstances we control oppose to the ones others lead us into.

My lane has been clustered with reckless and lane-swerving drivers who intentionally see me at a moderate speed – progressing faster than them rushing the bar across the speedometer. Some individuals are in their own lanes and most unfortunately their lanes are putting them through hell. It depends on what lane you choose, i.e. the program. Many will desire the fast lane; well keep in mind the fast lane brings you to situations and obstacles in your life a lot faster. Your results are coming to you a lot faster and how many people do you know accurately can hit a ninety-mile per hour fastball consecutively? Well, what did you think the fast lane was for? Speeding through life is rushing through all God has aligned for you to discover and learn from as an experience.

Passing these experiences by so fast, you come to the biggest roadblock in your lane and cannot even slow down to use what you know to get pass it. Your success is a lot longer sought for when you leave your lane, or try to go too quickly through your lane to reach your destination. Several of you have been working for years and it takes you a lifetime of age to accomplish what you should have accomplished years before. Do not allow yourself to become created from others and allow the ruthlessness of their existence to prey upon you. God is on twenty-four hour faith duty three hundred and sixty five days a year. You hold that faith in staying in your lane and God will constantly be working on your lane.

Intentionally positioned

CC

What focused topic do we actually study in search of finding reason? At that, what topics are studied in search of reason, and find indifference? Confusion builds from lack of consideration, not appreciation, but consideration.

What do we consider? Let me re-phase, what do we consider psychologically internally?

Without being acknowledged of how, information seeps into us like oxygen through pores. Information does more self-explaining than the poor excuse of a perception we gather; trying to neglect the fact information is why we have one. Concepts that are not constructed by topics we choose to focus on are the difference sustaining our ignorance to what makes change. By change I do not refer to physical characteristic alteration. Being informed and accepting what is informing, and also applying what information figuratively relative to what and who is informing, is knowledgeable action to creating the foundation of a perception likely to influence change. Information can be a dreamland destination far from the island of ignorance we isolate ourselves on.

Educated and attained knowledge is enough to re-distribute and collect concepts of the given information. Many see educated and assume school. Honestly, several of us, and I mean "us" as in all nationalities, will not make it through school. And, some of you may fall under the belief school is where you get educated.

NEWS FLASH it isn't.

School only determines how you will choose to be educated and where in your life you will be educated. You have heard of dropouts, well those dropouts are not as ignorant as you believe. To become universally educated the choice of consideration is in play. Information in schools will not reach those who do not consider taking it in – coincidently – whether you are in school or not. Education is in our thought and thoughts are preparations and these preparations determine outcome. Within thoughts we allow boatloads of information to be identified, thus creating the preparation.

Note: Identified is not the same as considered.

By simply knowing the information is there is as pointless as noticing a speeding car coming in your exact direction. Okay, you see it but then what? What else? Obviously, most of you would consider moving out of the way, and the motive being you do not want to get injured. Assume your knowledge of the reason allows you to know you will get hit, but you are absolutely ignorant to knowing you would get injured. Would a person still move out the way?

Of course they would but why?

Due to the person, while still ignorant to whether they would or would not be hurt, an individual would still consider getting hit in general i.e. fear of the unknown. Information focused upon a reason does not always prove most resourceful, due to it actually being a reason. Sometimes, it is just better to know to consider the action behind reason. To consider information is to accept it actually does exist. School, work, or even selling drugs you are going to intentionally force yourself into a position that can clearly be explained as failure. Limits are individually composed, and this act of limitation bars you from the information you could be considering sub-consciously.

When considering information, the process is always pondered as if it were a written manual for it. There is no secret or set way to consider information, you will just do it. One key word I want us to consider right now is a word I have been tossing around throughout my book.

"Interest"

Regardless of what we may want, or need, or dislike, and even hate: the supported incentive to have such feelings is through interest. And now, I expect you to stop being so mentally challenged – by intentionally positioning yourself into an act of showing lack of consideration.

Life is always flexing upon our flaws. Our minds need to open up to the information knocking with affirmation. Yes, I said knocking because information does knock and this is every time you witness the evidence of information being present. To just know the information is allowing you to build a city of your own perception, which can run as you grow to learn it can best function. Respectively speaking, with no insult intended, maybe the case as of today is that we have no city to populate with information. We have become so mentally challenged that we have lost the blueprint to a well functioning operation – city of thoughts – and have began winging it from day to day like a rebel migrating state to state without a social grasp on education. Bring to light that we are continuously falling into certain desperate needs of benefits year after year. Which is due to the original building plan that was well constructed for operation by God, being inconsiderably ignored.

I want all of you to remember the last time you spoke to someone you didn't know very well, and try to at least remember the conversation that was held. Now, many of us disregard the will power to consider, based off factors that can appear to be us avoiding unwanted situations in opposition to the idea of consideration, which eliminates certain factors for the sake of the prone possibility. This possibility being just because you have no interest or care to know does not necessarily mean you do not need to know. Read that last sentence over.

Be realistic, you have had an individual hold a well conversing moment with you, and your ideal thought was what the hell is this person talking about? Not only acknowledging obliviousness consciously but also sub-consciously you are informing yourself of how much you really care less to hear what the topic is.

Today, this is the lack of consideration that places us in situations later we find ourselves stressing over endlessly. Why?

There is a certain factor called "coincidence" and I believe coincidence is one of the keys you would find on a map to let you know what exactly you are looking at. Consider positioning yourself in a well awaited and worked for position at a certain point in your life. Once the time arrives for you to dwell in that accomplishment, one little informational situation evolves and creates a halt to the well-awaited moment of prosperity. Coincidence?

With that in mind, information we discuss daily brings us to the higher or lower learning positions, which we tend to only identify we are in after we fail somewhere somehow. Some individuals are learning and growing, and some are learning but not learning while they are learning. A sad fact but yet undeniably a reality because not learning while you are learning is a choice.

To learn and to learn and gain information is a choice we control by all means through our will power. With this control, the buttons may appear relative to a remote control but there is no play, pause, stop, or rewind and etc. There are actually three words with incredible capability to alter your living operation involved in this choice of learning. These words are actions and they are as follow:

Considering
Disregarding
Positioning

Three actions bringing your life to a certain intentional spot permitting you capability to consider what is available to you, and then position yourself where you plan and need to be. Or, you could simply disregard all three actions and attempt to position yourself where intentionally will be lacking information on how to get there. Which would you rather choose?

Of course we will finish reading the previous sentence and say we would rather consider. Yet, is it not reality that you only would choose considering because you were just made consciously aware.

You will say you would rather consider then position but the ultimate truth here is that the reason many of us are the way we are as people are because we are not considering anything without interest. We are disregarding without choice involved, and then we try to position ourselves in places that we are not considerably qualified to be in. The coincidence places a reality check on and in our lives and sends us to the window of opportunity displaying what we could of avoided, had we thoughtfully had the interest to consider, disregard, and position consciously.

We all are our own separate individuals evidentially, and life strikes many of us with a variety of similarities but also a multitude of great differences. One thing that I have noticed about us all is we all are trying to be ourselves but are not putting ourselves in positions to do so in a constructive advancing manner. We will say we are this and that and we like this and that, but the truth is it is just where we are intentionally positioning ourselves to be, do, and limit from becoming. That is a mental challenge, a real mental challenge that we can overcome.

Dementia is a condition where an individual's brain lacks function due to an associated disease. Dementia is also nonreversible. Memory and perception are two factors primarily affected when diagnosed with dementia. Cognitive skills are directly affected and as this information becomes one with your eyes, I want you to ask yourself, what option is there to consider, disregard, and position when you have no choice in either? We walk around living every day like we are what we believe we are, and in all actuality we know ourselves far to little to even attempt to be considerable with choice and without involved interest.

Many of us end up in conversations leading to arguments because we have intentionally placed ourselves there. Information is a tool of learning, with it you do not just learn about objects created or devices operated, but information can help us learn about ourselves in the moments we find most uninteresting. Some of you see others in there living patterns or situations and your outside comments are what was the point of that? Or, people do not think or the famous line of the last years:

"People are people"

Yes, they are people and the given proof to say this is directly observed through their actions. People are people and the challenge we all have mentally is that we cannot consider the idea that we are people but we are not naturally who we are designed to be. To be your own person, you can try to at least consider information about yourself by learning and knowing to be who you actually are even when it means accepting information you feel bears no relevancy to you directly.

Daily, many of us are making decisions that are the intent of our good and well being for the better outcome we either believe or can predict is coming or expected. A lot of us are making decisions with a mindset running off everything we have been through and what they are trying to prepare ourselves to go through. However, ask yourself, is everything you know based off experience everything you only need to know to live life progressively?

With all this in mind, still we are not giving ourselves time to consider how as a person we would be able to better ourselves in situations present, past reflected, and waited upon. The positions we are intentionally putting ourselves into are the ones we find ourselves stressing the most over – coincidentally.

You are going to find various ways you will and can be confronted by having self-conflicts with yourself, based upon your speech and your own actions. It brings you to a personal perspective where you look at yourself in a way that you are not, considering what you are like as the person you are now but still are not. We will continuously post pone the will to learn about ourselves while we learn about everything else that is around us, and furthermore put ourselves into a position where we speculate the idea, which is had we known ourselves better would we be able to handle certain situations better. Use what you have around you to become who you actually are and position yourself in a place where you mentally represent the person that you are. In our minds we can become everything in the world possibly known and thought of, yet, in our minds we also can become capable of understanding ourselves better with more comprehension of how we think and act without limiting ourselves to learning solely by intention.

NOTES:

CC

NOTES

What are we doing today?

"Do not cry because it is over now, laugh because it happened."

- Ceazzar Corleone

Ladies, forgive me but I am taking a direct shot at you today. My goodness what are we doing? Times are getting worse, and the progress of depression is exceeding and attacking a whole entire gender without light to shine on the issue. Ladies, the time to use what God has giving you would be this year, this month, and on this very day of this week, which you have decided to open this book and progress unto this chapter.

I sit down daily viewing the differences of the female character from one young lady to the next, and I witness many marvelous blessing from appeal to characteristics defining the soul. Yet, my curiosity has begun to question why such values of the character are still so rarely seen.

Let me be the first to say this is in no way a direct offense raising this issue to women. The honesty of our reality is screaming into the minds of our women, and a headache for me is an inner unanswered curiosity asking why are the values of a woman still being greatly ignored or overseen. There is a word to describe the actions females' train of thought displays that has the male race beat over all.

There is a skill that is perfected from birth and shown through every obstacle in life by a woman, but also poorly acknowledge do to a benevolent and devious act of emotion portrayed by man.

Women have been honored with the skill of responsibility. You all own it and have the perfection of its action embedded in your existence. It is magnificent how it just develops and how the priority alignment is stabilized to become managed in your life as a woman. The designs of your fluent acts of responsibility are the key, which many can never acknowledge until they open their soul unlocking the value of character. Many of us will never admit to our own acts of irresponsibility, but it is woman who has through extreme and sudden circumstances revealed the absolute definition of responsible.

Another thing I have observed very steadily is the ability of women to be on track about, and with, what they know. When most women have an idea of at least what needs to be accomplished and what they can accomplish, they will pursue such goal with irreversible drive. This perspicacious act evolves the will power, converting a basic understanding into a highly imperative made decision resulting in the following through of any devotion. The mind is a determined structure with beams of responsibility supporting it. The importance of having the ability to act responsibly is greater than simply knowing what to do, but not knowing if what to do is right or wrong and not accepting either as it is presented.

You can know what you are supposed to do but still be ignorant to how. Responsibility is commensurable to a how it can be accomplished manual. Women of past and present times have such a quality in them, and can advance the use of that quality far quicker. I stand witness to the capability and it can be heard it their tone of voice. It is amazing to me how the mind – when set to objectives – can balance out the responsibilities in accordance with the realities of any situation.

I can admit it and say it with no inferior presence that women are more responsible than men. And, here is where that statement loses its power. The truth of that statement is fading with the choices women are making today, and I am going to be honest with you ladies, many of your choices are poor, poor as the eighteenth hundred lower class living. Many of you read that and are immediately sounding a defensive sentence which may say:

"Oh no, men make way more poor decisions than women." Guess what ladies... NO SHIT!

CC

The obviousness of man's poor decision-making skills needs no research and the argument is evidentially pointless to debate. The reality of how shocking a woman's decision-making skills have become is worth debating. Ladies, the world is run for you, and you can be realistic, and after the tables turn the real story trickles down into the fact most of the power and money is attained to satisfy the requirements of a lady, when in attempt to pique her. America is unconsciously spinning to achieve the approval of your desires of living, why masking man's most unjustified ambitions over it. We do everything for women because after all the power struggles and money measuring to judge an individual – and that is not by his character but his wallet and position of authority in life, we want the one thing women provide best in this world, and that is love and responsibility.

The universal focus and goal embedded deep within us connecting us most – from one soul to the next is love, and while most will argue power, 1 will argue that power is the façade substituting for love in areas where there is lack there of. While power is still up for debate, however, in contribution to keeping us justifiably together – power is less likely the big deal to bear our greater concerns upon.

Why do men care about how they dress? Why do men care about how they look? What car they drive? Or, how they live and where they live?

The irreversible reality and unmasking truth is a woman and the love she can express fluently and in unsurpassable amounts, which mends families together and households into orthodox living styles. The denial of man is a reflection of pride in disguise seeking disclosure from the truth. That is the reality that behind eyes and in the mind are only recognized by those who refuse to ignore it. The image is clear, and those guys who argue that their will power to provide care for themselves is simply due to power, are wrong.

Power to a man ensures that he will receive a multitude of rewards without challenge to his request. Women are at times trapped in the process of this misconception. Thus, ladies your poor decisions are influencing the cynicism of your skill to be more responsible, unfold into the evidence of a hoax fact. We may continue this argument by asking how are your decision-making skills that awful?

Well, you are letting the development and creativity of various levels of emotions to devour the internal chamber locking away what keeps you sane. Or, in other words what holds in the sanity of love deep inside you, is constantly in jeopardy of being eradicated from your soul.

Love and Trust

Keeping everything you hold in during unstable circumstances and in the very moments you feel life breaking apart, is why your love and responsibility to love in areas of life many find difficult, you will find possible. As of today, ladies you are giving up the blessings God has placed inside of you to reveal the plan and purpose involved with it.

Mentally, you are allowing emotions to be taken from you and they are what keep you in connection to the world. Do not allow yourselves to be deprived of your remarkable insight, and also do not allow the controversial skepticism placed around how you express yourself, to be captured by circumstances you are strong enough to overcome.

Relationships are popping up everywhere like a contagious outbreak consuming all who breath. The standards of mentally focusing on love as the primary priority can increase by the emotional value you place on a situation. Knowing that let me ask you one question.

CC

Who in this world besides God should be more important than you?

Consider the emotional channels you have flipped through throughout your life, and as well various levels of emotional climbing – up and down between different and even permanent moments in your life – moments crossing trust and love. Every day I see the same relationships and types of relationships again and again failing to succeed in understanding each other. Ladies you are a golden gift in most, if not all, categories in life. You obtain the equality of everything even when unseen.

Placing your mind into a perception that can open a door to obvious self-destruction can describe the damage you are doing to yourselves when you give out your trust like charity. Today, there are too many women sexually active outside of trust and emotion. There are far too many women allowing love to lead them into a dysfunctional process of thinking and thought recycling patterns.

Take some time to stare at your own reflection, and as it displays everything you are, close your eyes and look into your personality and find what makes you divine and extraordinary, as well as what makes you flawed and uncompromising.

It is 2013 and the reality of man's devious and careless capability to use their emotions has infiltrated your purpose. Knowing this ladies, you must not still tangle your emotions into these characters with their description printed in plain view. Ladies, you are not keeping your emotion at the highest peak of its value. You are capable of loving perfectly; well of course no one is perfect so let us say 99.9% and save that one percent for critics to make a point on.

Then again, some of you ladies avoid love like fear inspires the evidence of its presence, so let's say 95.9% of you are capable of loving perfectly. Actually, we may have to just do 90%, but ok whatever – you know what I am trying to say. The love a woman can give any being on this earth will be powerful enough to keep lights on if it took only a kiss on a fuse box. A woman's ability to love great can cause any man to become the most determined, honest, and loyal individual. Unfortunately, like most great features of the world around us, a woman's love is also being taking advantage of. The tendency to over abuse the positives most fortunate to us in life are prone to the behavior of mankind. All I ask is that you learn what can become and what cannot become, and how to determine the two skillfully.

Embrace your capabilities as an individual and a woman, and seek the inner purpose of the advantages blessed upon you in the form of an emotional ability. Take time to grow and learn what you are capable of giving out, and how you giving it out can be most affective. I truly believe the time to act on your realization of what can and cannot stand is now. Self-respect is an imperative accessory necessary to utilize your ability to love.

A large number of women are taking a nosedive into the deception that man has ignorantly created. Reality has now become a more aggressive image manipulated to assist in the continuation of programs in life. I have reached out to many of my peers from little sisters, big sisters, and women in general. And, those who know me know what I encourage: maintain focus, focusing on yourself, and what you can innovatively design yourself into. Men are not leaving this earth anytime soon, they will be here tomorrow and next week, a month from now, and decades from then.

Understand you can learn the skill you possess in responsibility and use it to your advantage when distributing your love.

My highest encouragement can only be directed towards young lady's and women who have a sense of attentive intention to find their inner self, and study that area in hopes to form an understanding of their personal value. The road to developing yourself into a well-characterized young lady is only but through listening and wanting to understand what can be understood. The information to research such value is placed in front of you daily. Seriously, the women of today are not getting any hidden exposure, if you as a woman degrade yourself, men are not hiding their will to display that you are capable of being degraded openly and publically.

I want women to understand that the world basically generates to comfort you. Picture a world without your presence, the essence of love would be absent and deserted and likely never sought for after eradication. Focus not on the fact there are countries supporting religions, which find an unequal existence in the lifestyles of women. Still, the negligence does not have to oversee the sunken truth in other locations on earth.

It is as if the road to being, becoming something better has everything laid out but the true knowledge behind the fact is removed as quickly as it is realized. Ladies all you have to do is learn, learn to develop yourself from the inside out and on the outside reflect the loving nature without fear of the mistakes or intentional actions of man. Stressful situations will stack on you because you are a woman, and God wants you to decisively accept the understanding of how to be a woman, which will compel you to become strong, confident, and unconditionally caring with purpose. This significant fact can always be made obvious; that you are capable of passion. Passion has its tragedies and can make its mistakes, misleading – but ultimately passion can recreate a world of elegance. Take for instance, many men are working for money, and not just men in general but many people are doing what they do for a living for money obviously. There is nothing behind labor but material results and an unfair expectation of acquiring resources, and this is to be believed the cycle of survival. Women will always be great successors, due to the fact they can provide passion to any craft, in a way it connects their ambition to their ability in one synchronized understanding.

A lot of you are going to be introduced to sex very early, and some of you at an age so ridiculously early, I'd highly support the idea that America is losing control of its children. The act itself is a tool to break the woman out of you young ladies early. When I said break I mean break and not bring. See, the idea is break because when a woman loses her virginity she is broken from a form of spiritual purity. Even with grown women, I am still trying to figure out why we put an age on everything that is not law or ruled. The sexual experiences of younger women are growing into a massive case of early encounters, with little knowledge and more ignorance to why they actually perform it. Some younger women are being misled by a feeling that can be completely eradicated by the simple acknowledgment of what makes you who you are. To know yourself is to know what you can control and the feelings, which sneak up on us often, being controlled by your knowledge of your value. We all form feelings for that extraordinary person, the one who influences us to feel as though we are touched uniquely by what never really matters, which would be attraction. And my young queens, the more you know what really matters the more what doesn't matter at all can be fundamentally avoided.

I know, you like this guy and he seems nice and is everything you find attractive, but the last thing you want him to be is a thief. It sounds beautiful, but I am not asking women to avoid their will to love or their passion to love, or even to escape the habitually course of having sex. I am just asking young ladies to actually take the time to sit down and analyze what can be researched, and thus furthermore understood so that you are not being broken into but by will brought out of.

Here is my example before I close this chapter out, take a good second and think about anybody you have ever dealt with on a personal yet extreme emotional level. Now, hear me and think but do not speak with me, and do not try to establish your own reasoning. Please just try to think as you read.

Past relationships that were not emotionally successful – when you begin the interest into someone you acknowledge what can be absolutely stunning – are likely because you must ask yourself what is beautiful about a person, as well what are the resembling perfect like qualities that person may portray. Now, we see these factors and base our emotions into a level that cautions us of what nice presence these qualities can carry, and how these qualities should be respectfully carried out.

Those nice qualities provide a barrier for negativity and keep you focused on the positives. Many relationships will halt at the break of tolerance between one or both parties. As this tolerance is collapsing, the reconstruction process goes through everything but what got you started emotionally in the first place. We always accept what qualities last in the visual but never keep them when they disappear, and we never remember them. The time to be yourself is when you are with someone else who is finding out what about you are the most incapable thing for him or her to bear with. Being you is how we always go into situations, and out of character is how we typically come out.

Be yourself and learn for yourself and create a self-perspective concept idea that respect has its presence in the upbringing of your womanhood. I say all this to conclude, a woman who has develop herself as a woman from the inside out, will stand a better fighting chance at withstanding the negative and senseless traps designed and set up by man's illusive feeble mind. What are we doing today? Are you becoming a strong young woman growing into a full adult with self-respect inspiring you to exclusively protect your value?

Man needs love; love is the connection from one human being to the next that also connects us to God. Women can provide this love with a mature and innovation mind leading a strong and dedicated responsible heart. Ladies when I ask what are we doing today?

One of the target challenges I quickly want to focus on is how man can hinder the expression of a woman's love. Over time there have been a growing number of men who cannot keep their hands to themselves. Whether it is due to their history of rage or the fact they cannot get their way so they use their power. Regardless, this unnecessary act is cause many women to reflect on love differently and recite it cautiously.

If a man places his hands on you even once, I assure you with all the blood pumping through my veins, he will do it again. Once a man activates this behavior you have no choice, just leave. Evacuate the premises, or, call the police and have the individual removed. If you have children and you feel as though he is unfit to parent alone, then you began researching into beginning a custody case. This will be a fight to begin but it is worth fighting for the sake of your safety and others around you.

Stop allowing these men to hit you and scorn you with fear, so much that you once removed by the grace of God from that predicament, are not convinced it is love responsible for your dismay. Love does not make a man crazy, but it is negativity and hatred, foul thoughts and evil within leaving God with out, which creates a bad man. Love is soulful and full of God's joyful music. Love is not the enemy neither is it the influencer of evil. People who love with the love God has inspired – like the love in women – are not tamed by demons and the thoughts alike.

Ladies you must understand that your mental challenged is your inability to activate your love. Expressing your love is significant to the survival of mankind. Recreating life is a possibility because of the love within that through God you can activate and begin becoming apart of a changing society. The lies about love and the joy improperly stationed around sins is an anomaly. Love is the key, and when you are thinking to yourself, when you are listening to that voice compatibly discussing how you feel with what you feel. That is the real power of a woman working within you to discover the values inside and make use of them with the values outside. Feel no fear for your ability to love strong. Yet, I will say it starts in the mind, as you are only going to make yourself wiser, stronger, and able by thought inspired belief.

I'd like to know many of you will respond with working on you to become who God designed you to be, in great hopes to share responsibly the values of your love nation and world wide.

Moving a Mind

"We seldom think of what we have, but we always think of what we miss."
- Ceazzar Corleone

The mind is a possible exit from reality, presenting doorways of explanations you sole find excusable for what reality consistently puts in front of you.

I envision more ways of passionate expressions being acceptable to the mind just as much as many other people. And saying that, I ask where do we feel most comfortable expressing our emotions?

Do we take personal time into consideration, using that time to ourselves when we are alone to discover our emotional side?

The sight of emotional release is a captured moment, showing emotional expressions we are capable of and where they were created. So delicate is the act of spreading feelings, even when the feeling is self supported as you sync in the energetic force behind your feelings shooting them off into the universe.

Care or concern is the reaching arm into your pocket not putting money in but neither taking money out, just checking to make sure money is in there. Some of us are very determined to let others know how we feel, while others are not so easily on display, seeking more comfort in hiding out their emotions from the universe – or so they believe they do.

Outlets, which are methods we use to express, are curiously pondered over as feelings begin to set into our realm of energy within and around our soul.

One particular thing we all may forward with our actions over our words is the will to be independent. Many of us are putting our lives into perspectives that create an environment we only know how to survive in alone. In alternative, it may fit the world today but we all can say the world today even needs a change beyond one individual's independent state of mind.

The passion of independence births from the idea it can secure success faster and solidify an

CC

individuals status of life. That at no point can appear bad or tardy, but once again, alternatively the seeking of independence contributes to the poverty and the struggling.

Take for instance the ambition you apply into the proliferation of your life's opportunities. This ambition may not necessarily be to succeed, but you may just have your wants in the front and are letting them lead you with the idea of results you seek to attain. It creates a position, which you then make yourself feel that you are chasing a value that cannot be measured with others opinions. It sounds almost as if the will to succeed has been well influenced by being sought individually.

This idea, or theory has today traditionally been influenced as we gather examples to believe the idea is a fact. Quite true on the contrary that even if the help was provided for someone's ambition, some may still come to see that their independence can be challenged less. Some of us force our intentions with the urge to prove or justify some point of view we feel the need to defend or express. Quite like myself, as of now I see that I have waited for help for a very long time, and have been still waiting until this day. In the midst of my waiting, I have found myself supported with more reasons to be independent than uniting with some group of resourceful partners, and aim for a big goal. It almost seems as if I were being lead by others neglect to be independently focused. Sounds weird right?

Well, the part of the mind that can be influenced is not exactly my field of study, but what I have analyzed from our behavior is what can only be described as what moves our minds. Minds are being moved, and they are being pushed by reasons supported from inside and outside patterns of obstinate parties. In a second, I will elaborate. You will not understand this challenge until you completely finish this book, but I will provide the pieces to develop an understanding of what needs to be understood.

MENTAL CHALLENGE: Moving a mind

Today, we sub-consciously perceive sides of us that are created from the environment we live in, and as well the company that surrounds us i.e. friends, family, etc. The environment and company, influentially supports actions we pursue in response to sudden experiences in life. This act of perceiving cannot be indicated unless our eyes are not in our own sockets. Inevitably impossible, let's try to pin point this concept from a metaphoric position of sight.

We all go to work for what we need and want, clock in and out and back in after that less than eight hours of sleep has passed over. A lot of us have talents and some may entertain them for fame, while others will pursue the joyful expression of their skill for the love of it. If you would like a greater example of what I am trying to say, take men for the prime of example. Several – if not all – men do almost everything for something and that is completely disregarding the idea they consider what really matters.

Are you ready?

I will warn you now, this is my book and I can say what I want and with that said, this is not in order but cars, money, jewelry, clothes, and the most significant necessity for all men – a woman are all incentives for man's every growing desire to breathe. As a matter of fact, men will value anything they want possession of, especially power!

Above are the primary values of man – perhaps values of a man whose mind has been tampered with by society much more than it has been encouraged by wisdom – which is being disclosed to help you realize that something's will always move the mind, to force the incentive influencing intention to act or behave. The life we live today is built around the influenced values moving our minds. I witness every day citizens spend loads of money on tennis shoes or some form of fashion, I have witnessed many words leave the mouths of men and women – and either their words are to ameliorate above the situation that we rest in, or they are what we may just want and want more frivolously. The conditions of our minds are being influenced by what moves us attentively and attractively but only to poison us sub-consciously. I watched the actions of those around me become vivid examples for determining how a mind can be moved uncontrollably.

This process of moving can go as simple as consuming food, you eat food due to the fact you are hungry, which is true by all means, but wait. Few of us eat due to the fact we seen something that we wanted to try and have this feeling of curiosity. The hunger is there but hardly ever the particular motive, or else we could have just ate something and not feed the curiosity of our mind influencing our tongue.

Curiosity is actually the incentive for a lot of our minds being moved today. Oh you think different, well, do you actually believe when you see celebrities in movies, or music artist performing, and you begin to imagine it is you performing or acting a role on stage or in a hit movie that you are not being curious? You are completely curious to the idea of being such. All of us have had our "what if's". That is curiosity at work and at time this curiousness can create incentive and that incentive can make its way to move our minds. It is clear our minds can be moved, and will continue to be moved by the result of interest and curiosity.

The challenge is allowing uncontrolled interest and appeal to negatively influence the unorthodox coordination of how we handle our priorities, thus moving our minds selectively for us and not us moving our minds through will power. As simple as this may sound or some, the simple part of this is actually as complicated as it does not look. Do not let the words on this page befool you, a mind moved by routine is an issue, especially when the moving incentive is the leading cause of what can be explained as what society looks like today. Your eyes are a window to everything you can walk into, and still we keep the curtains closed only to reopen when influence and instructed by forces other than our own. Humor is, the reason we become so moved by nothing, which should be actually valued is the fact we are allowing it to move us without the consideration of any value. Anything you let move your mind – will, and for as long as you permit it.

I find the reason many of us have insecurities with social company is from us being moved into independent intentional non-spiritual train of thought(s). Our thoughts are being processed with the independent intention; never available are other areas of expertise or advisory when a mind is cycling throughout this state. This is the creation of our own will to avoid acknowledging what can be acknowledged and taken advantage of. Learning is fundamental and experimental to the brain, and also significant to the mind becoming a better-developed tool for thinking. Of course, learning what and when appears as a debate with fate, being as though we all are acknowledging facets of life with our own lives at the fate of our own responsibility. And, I ask what makes you so sure?

The will to provide and help is the ability to create any possible difference and change. A mind moved awkwardly and without knowledge of will power can produce the reasons we see no change and have no effect, even on one individual untapped mind. Given the opportunity, we still avoid being moved by what can be a motivational recreating formula for a troubled mind. Believe me when I say we are going too far, and we have gone beyond far with what is improperly valued. As a result, we create our own struggle within the current struggle life already serves us. This mixture is without identification, irreversible.

Some of you have read this far into my book and still do not understand the purpose of my book. It is not a fault to misunderstand, but only because you cannot misunderstand what I am telling you. Your mind is being moved by your own actions but influenced by other parties other than your own will. This chapter is actually allowing you to see what I saw. Our minds are being moved; Uhual'd to the perception of misunderstanding ourselves through societies influences, creating this need for wants as oppose to our instinctual want for needs. Learning this is the spark igniting inspiration to what can be rearranged into a mind valuing the qualities of who we are, and then abolishing the state of thinking causing us to be ruled over and inspired with falsified values.

Now this stretches far, a mind can be moved to the point where interest is even imposed. Thought to believe, the like is love and love is now the obsessed. Why do you think many of us think independently about our own lives?

We all do and still due to the struggle never changing and the days – which constantly do – however do not let time of day fool you. A second can move fast but our actions and thinking minds can pause and pause so instantly either may move without the other. This pausing will happen the moment we try to contain what moves our mind. Why?
We are taking control of what can and possibly has the most advantage of value over our life. These are our moments where we are realizing we have a choice. And, this choice is to use our will power to control how we move our own minds.

Many will only read to find the examples of what can be related to the obviousness of life, simply practical universal points, which can serve the purpose of controlling parties as well as parties broken free.

Life is so much more than bills and payments
and fussing and fighting with others debating reason
and authority abusing every right given and taken away.
We all are continuing to live with situations of life that
bring us confusion and misunderstanding, and at times
the frustration of shutting others out is a welcomed
idea by society. Society wants you to shut each other
out, because that means you all cannot work together,
and if you are not working together why would you
help another, or reality is you would not. Try to see
what I have seen from us to some extent, our actions
and words are examples for what we can use to find
ourselves better circulating thought patterns, which we
control as we grow and learn of the needs we ought to
favor.

Why should anyone feel as though a person can
be fearfully skeptical of someone's company?
It is as if individuality has brought a selfish
feeling to fill a room of unlimited capacity. Of course
we watch our company we keep and this is true as of
today we should. Alternatively, with the idea of knowing
whom you are individually – accept that everyone else
knows we can advance by cooperatively understanding
the negatives of independent moved minds, and if they
do not know, you know now to inform them.
One thing we have to understand is that the
world is full of information that is organized to tear
your life into nothing. Many of us receive insight and do
not want it to flourish as our new understanding. The
actual act of consideration would be to take in
knowledge, align it with your own, and thus create a
universal concept. I think it's sick that we can become
more obligated to ourselves and in the end everyone is
still struggling together. Instead, we all are being moved
to believe we can individual beat struggle.

I just find it outrageous that our minds can be
impressed with what has no effect on the future of our
existence – together. Our minds are challenged with

the task of learning, and what we choose to learn has been built into the complications of life as we live, and this solidifies the opportunity to take control of your progressing mind. It is as if we believe that the times of change are coming by the changes we make ourselves. Partially true, I realized myself even with the accomplishments one can make, change will and can come quicker with me and others succeeding together, vice versa, me succeeding and watching or waiting for others to succeed after me.

Recognize, the change you make by yourself is not ignored or unappreciated, but the change you make with another individual is twice the ground covered, and ten times more with others involved.

You may ask yourself why am I focusing on change and help, well look at our cycle of struggle. There are three levels of living – in their eyes and understanding, surviving – and a lot of us are right in between the middle class and poverty level. Even though, today it is no shy idea that many people are merging the two levels into one. Those individuals in the positions many of us work to be in have been mentally moved to the training and learning's, which inspire the true rewarding results of achieving cooperatively with other people.

What do you think is going on in the world, everyone is getting it how they live but individually. Yes it feels that way to us. On the other hand, up the ladder many of us fail to climb in due time of our average life span, there is actually a communist society living above a capitalism controlled society.

We is an expression of the levels merged into an insane formality we call surviving. We are being controlled; they are working together to control us. We are the only ones with our challenges and are allowing these challenges to cripple us into an indefinite struggle. Those so called, leaders in high places have got there with the help of others in the highest of places before them. What they will not and do not teach you is how to work together to get ahead, and then bring the next class of aspiring workers into the next level you and others have progressed into. Your thoughts are moving within a fugue state of mind, this emboldens the presupposition entitling you to a set routine, which is over seen by rule makes who neither have to abide by the rules they make, nor stalk the cycle they spin.

Please understand, it is not only about a mind being moved to believe that being in a high place is where life becomes grand and dandy. The idea of success is only what any man perceives it to be for him. When the influence of trained methods of "Survival" are implicated into a routine, there is not much light shinning over a natural vision of success. The high place life style is not as many of us say, where it is at, and this is where I can elaborate, as I so eagerly want to on this topic.

Our minds are being moved to believe we have to work to achieve goals that are going to get us into high places, yet these high places are only embracing values and formalities, they have set rules and laws – insensible to the idea of revealing such processes, which function evidentially successfully. Every high place is not where we need to be in order to live. Take the sky for instance, the higher you get the air gets thinner because air pressure decreases nearly thirty percent since the atmosphere becomes less dense. This makes it harder for you to breathe at higher altitudes causing oxygen to have trouble entering our cardiovascular network. I do not want you to mistake this for a psychological attack, because this also applies to those who feel as though they are achieving to get in the low places that have high place benefits.

You are not advancing like you believe you are no matter how high or low you go. Take the ocean for instance, the lower you go the water pressure increases. Water has weight and as you ascend deeper into the ocean, you are putting more water on top of you, causing more pressure to be exerted from you. In brief

CC

conclusion, going too low will affect you just as much as going to high.

There is no advantage about being the get over type personality, and neither is there an advantage for being I can do it myself and for myself achiever. Given the reader support, I would like many of you right now to begin thinking what is the last thing that you did in general and why you did it? Use the first thing that comes to your mind. And now, do not consider the reason you have done it, but the reason why you will continue to do it.

Remember what you allow to move your mind will move your mind. This is evidential as we continue to live our lives in routine. They influenced logic is that we must survive. Our realistic goal should never be to fight for your life that you were never placed here to fight over. Our responsibility is to live, and as we live we find our purpose, recognize the plan, and after example the idea of living your life.

Continuously we are persuaded through entertainment markets, and some of our most unforgivable seven deadly sins. They program makers have take the sins and marketed them into our lifestyles, and they have done so because it is written in word that we will indefinitely and forever sin. Sin is what we will do, and every deadly sin is being marketed around us to profit a system of forwarding kill or be killed ideas into the minds of many individuals who simply want to live. It is in our nature to feel the need to live. It is no mistake to believe you should and are able to. Yet, we do not have to live so broken by rules that only regulate us into personal, social, and financial battles with each other.

Your mind is a powerful force of resting energy constantly shooting off sparks of identity. Every inner voice, and indecisive decision is your mind fighting the influenced ideas cripple society. We can control the movement of our mind as we begin to understand exactly what are the installed ideas. Training is mandatory and meditation plays a major role in converting installed ideas into natural sense of learning. Innovative can become the adjective surrounding other praised qualities encouraging how we process our thoughts.

Life has many specific ideas that have been prepared and trained into society, and I could individually get into a lot of them but I beg you to immediately begin tapping into your mind. Begin to track your train of thoughts to locate those invading ideas of how to live life. When you are living your life, and however you may live it, just begin to think about what is catching your attention, what you are often reading, and whom you are often around or surrounded by.

I cannot tell you what should or should not move your mind, while we all possess similar characteristics and qualities, we all do have unique values within our minds. I can however help you understand how to realize that you own the choice when determining what moves your mind, and how you can continue to move your mind willingly enforcing the values of living with a purpose.

CC

Listening

To open your ears almost sounds idiotic based
off the actual fact that your ears never close. Well,
what if I am not referring to the ears that are located
aside you cranium. I am instead referring to the ears in
your mind; the ones that are allowing the information
in and out like boarder line security. We are oblivious
to the fact we can decide what we want to listen to
sub-consciously. And, now that I am on the topic let us
ask the question:

What do you choose to listen to and why?

Answer:

This is an easy answer for the mind of an
individual who is not stressing the act of thinking too
hard. Of course, in most cases we only listen to what
we like in light of the benefit to our self-improvement
as an individual. In other words, we will continue to
allow our ears to hear solely based off interest. Sounds
silly if you ask me, but one person allowing information
from all over to be determined – how useful it can be
by that person's interest, might be constructively the
best learning solution. I have been tossing the word
interest all over this book, and many of you should have
already established the connection between interest and
the mental challenges of life. Forgive me if I am giving
some of you too much credit, however, the interest we
permit to rule over our decision making process is what
causes us to lead ourselves poorly with information we
mentally hear. Information is to be of value, and to
understand the value of anything is to comprehend the
reality of its existence, not only in your life but others
around you.

The road to a city called understanding is
always going to have detours, and these detours are
basic to complex levels of information.

Off topic, but by now you may have also
noticed the relevant simile connecting roads and
beltways and cities to actual life experiences. This only

CC

due to the fact these factors act as the best examples in my opinion. Always, when you can, recognize metaphors for life. I learned this listening to two men who have very conscious minds well developed with understanding the values of their experiences in life. To conclude, it took me listening to them in order to understand this tactic I just suggested.

Most of us are on a journey to become something that we want to be or just something better than what we know we unsatisfactory and evidentially are. Strange enough, we dare embark on these journey's still unwilling to accept the idea, which is there can be information we may not like to hear or read that is the most valuable to us. I am not sure how many of my readers are well experienced in living life, but life is full of so much experience we avoid learning from, and thus preventing us from capitalizing on information within these experiences designed to recreate our train of thinking. These experiences can make us better than we want to be or worst than we ever could imagine ourselves becoming. The ears within our mind are going to determine how we develop through life; this is the type of challenge where we fail to comprehend our ability to successfully comprehend universally and responsibly that which we endure.

The earful challenge

First things first, this mental challenge is pretty self-explanatory, but in all actuality the incontestable fact is that many of us are just poor ass listeners. And, before I grab my shovel – my keyboard – and type in these identifications, I would like you to take a second to understand some learning disabilities.

Learning disabilities are more than likely described as mental restrictions prohibiting the full expression of natural born abilities. While most learning disabilities are not diagnosed until the child has entered school, some of these disabilities are nonetheless established at birth. Now, a disability can be anything from hyperactivity to problems with writing, reading, and math. Now that we have squared away that informational fact, I would like for you to ask yourself how do we learn to read, write, and control our emotions, actions, and decisions.

The point I am making is that, we must first listen to learn, process to install, and reflect to progress with our learning's. Reflection is the moment you recite what you have installed and apply it to the current events you are enduring. In order to do this as effectively as requisite, you must tap into your sub-conscious thought process and listen to your ideas and memories recycling throughout your mind. Your thoughts will become willing to the demands of your mental ears. As soon as you call on certain thoughts containing various forms of information, your mind begins to prepare that information like a projector in a classroom before students take notes. Significantly identified, listening is the part of this process we must entertain with great practice.

Processing information stands out on many of you as a look as you are listening. You may wonder how listening can have a look, but it does have an actual appearance. I am referring to the looks that you display after the information was shared. All of you right now consider someone who has given you advice about any event or situation in your life, which today has assisted in molding you into who you are today. Think about what happened in your life that caused you to feel like you needed the information, and next determine what you received as given information, and finally what did you do to openly prove that the information you were given was poorly accepted and appreciated.

Point being you realized that someone advised you of information, and you still neglected the use of the information and the consideration of it. However

CC

your actions displayed this would be the look of a poor ass listener.

Listening is actually difficult for many of us who are far too occupied considering our actions externally to actually lend our ears to others. Unarguably you listen with your hearing ears, but what about your ears that control the in and out transportation of information. Those ears are programmed by interest and causing the misconceptions of what should be heard and what can be heard. There should never be a point where you are allowing what comes into your mental ears to be programmed – by all means it should be manually operated.

How to Manually operate your mental ears:

Have you ever been so anxious to do something that you thought of doing it and were so ready to pursue it but at the moment the action can be pursued, you stop and think about whatever it is that could possibly change your mind? You are now considering information. As you consider information, you are analyzing the choice you have and in fact, you are even at times giving yourself a choice in general. Take for instance men, when it comes to women men have allowed them to be the ruler of their thoughts. Why?
Interest. Pure interest.

Man's interest in women gives man no organized choice, favorably when a guy has seen a female his mind completely focuses on the ideal thoughts of what can come to mind, in most cases sex. At times, a guy may feel the need to speak to a female for preoperational purposes as he instigates a formal or less than savvy entrance into conversation. Other times, some guys may be reserved and refuse to engage on their thoughts. Such thinking is uncontrolled and debatably instinctual. Behavior of the sort conflicts with the transportation of information, and also impedes on the delegation of any understanding corresponding to the next.

With men – in a general relationship of course – man's introduction of his personality to a female is at most disrespectful and not needed in various cases. A guy may introduce himself because of interest; yet, the programmed processer being interest without control cannot be forwarded into the train of considerable thoughts. Now at times, guys may see a female and want badly to introduce themselves, but will reserve their speech unknowledgeable of the information, which reminds them of the lady they already have. At that moment, a guy will have taken the programmed interest – responding ears, and control them manually. Allowing information that is valuable to be useful in the time of need to understand and collect his thoughts of reality. Complicated at best, nonetheless this is not an overly extensive effort when in the process of choreographing a scene in your mind to correlate with your other thoughts.

What we do many times over is let the information we currently know run over the information we have to acknowledge, which is stored but not properly placed to be effortlessly located. The task we make hard for ourselves is when we help ourselves believe information we need to acknowledge is always and only heard. Your mental ears during this error will become your complex solution. It is the most awful way to listen when we believe that we have to listen to someone else to learn. Realize my challenged friends' listening; again it is not always what you hear from others that will enhance your current state of thinking. Not even what you read from others. What you hear or read from yourself will always serve you as the best resource for learning. The moment you learn from yourself, you are training your mind and preparing it to learn from others.

By opening the ears within your mind you allow what information you have naturally acquired to live in the act of being useful. Many of you have had conversations with each other and the topic at first seems too dull to add your input. Eventually, after listening with the ears in your mind you will find that the information you are hearing is neither new nor learned but recognized. This is why one of the most difficult challenges for us today is being capable of listening. Listen to what you know. The way to listen is only difficult when we find the aggravation in believing that listening is for the ears located outside.

No one really wants to hear others talk, and especially with people we are not familiar with. The idea of hearing what they have to say is rarely adored, unless the interest is entertained. I am asking you to manually control your mental ears so natural interest is inspired and can clutch onto the information others can and will provide.

It almost seems as if they can hear me...

Yes we can, and we are listening all the time. When you talk to yourself I am sure you have sub-consciously thought can they hear me? Many of you are probably thinking I am requesting you to just talk to yourselves. Leaving you with the humiliation of appearing to be a sad soul burdened to be isolated to you being your only friend. Call me crazy and strap me in because I am demanding that you begin talking to yourself more often. And if you are staring into the beautiful nothingness at the moment, I want to interrupt your wonderment to inform you this is the most effective form of listening you can conduct. It can seem quite extraordinary when you are listening to the most important person besides God in your life, you. That would be you; I am sure someone looked both ways and started scratching their heads. Yes, I am still referring to you.

The personal information you keep to yourself you only identify when you are remembering when the event has place of relevance to today. Right well actually the event has place every day. In fact almost everything you experience your mind listens to and collects the information. The reasons some things you are incapable of instantly discovering you know are because you choose to not listen.

Your ears within the mind are begging for your attention. They are begging because your mental ears know you have a program running your thoughts in a cycle that gives them so much useless information, and limits your ears to put out so little. Listening is a great talent to acquire. It is the mental development of understanding and realizing new, old, constant, and alternate techniques to customize your learning capabilities.

We can create a better understanding of what we like and dislike, are prone to agreeing with, and are more than likely going to disregard while being knowledgeable of it all. Imagine, you can possess the capability to know yourself so well you are then capable of listening to others because you have made it known to yourself the interest you control and put out, so you can bring information in.

Listening can tell you not only why you like any particular noun but also if you should like it. I listen to people all the time and many of them talk with the intent to explain while some speak with the intent to advise; yet all of us speak with the intent to be heard. On a serious note, who speaks without wanting to be heard? No one. You would not want to sit or stand expressing your views and as you do everyone is passing by without the slightest concern. We fail to listen to ourselves and thus fail to understand how to effectively listen to others.

CC

I once ignored a person talking to me for about an hour. Completely said to myself, I do not want to hear this person speak. I was not interested and thought solely about some other topics, which I felt an interest for. However, the individual speaking was discussing some offensive point of views, because of this I shut out what they were physically saying, and processed the information in my mind to determine they need to shut out but consider their information.

I was not listening with my ears, but I was listening with my mental ears. Paying attention to neglect attention was the case. The person was wrapping up the topic of discussion. At the end of their discussion, I was capable of fully comprehending their perspective while also being able to negate the offensive nature of their conversation. This is a dire process of organizing thoughts, which can be done by listening with your mental ears. The biggest challenge with listening is that we force ourselves to take in information in bulk, when it can be broken down, so we can further take what's relevant and disregard what is not.

Open up!

Realize

CC

Our days are burdened. Struggle is fencing in every individual like a full body suit suppressed against the body. It is impossible to feel untouched by a stressful massage coming from your personal masseuse – struggle. Struggle affects us in a way we have grown to live with, almost as if there is an entrance without an exit. The air is intoxicated with misunderstandings of what accepting struggle can bring to light. Various misconceptions surface as the numbers increase in individuals becoming content with their routine trials.

Some of us have accepted struggle and continuously fail to see behind the curtain. Many are just zoning, working, and venturing to places with the expectation of comfort as if the stress that grooves the texture of their life is that smooth.

Accidents/mistakes become traditional and actions are inevitably made routine, and the results of our troubles will be bargain with to an extent it develops its own mask over the original layer of reality. I believe constant blind misconception is where we find depression burgeoning into our lives. As we began to bargain with struggle allowing it to be accepted into our lives, we unconsciously consistently deflect the original reality of living life in a less than controlled manner. Choosing struggle is at the deal of your efforts, and as a result you are creating the acceptable links connecting your anxiety to the ideal expressions of tardiness. Meaning you will become lazier because you become more content.

Reacting to this misconception, attempt to gain the balance in struggle, which you still see an advantage in advancing out of struggle through further efforts. The advantage you believe you have is going to be being capable of managing your life mentally in the stride of struggle. We play with our mind by day dreaming how we desire our life actively out of struggle.

Drawing mental images of what we would do, or what we want to do, these images with the comfortable lights are shining on you keeping you out of the darkness of struggle. You are building in your head the wants and needs for your life vividly and almost as if possible, and they are possible. Acceptance allows the mind to venture a road only seen behind the eyes never in front of them. Problems are continuously constant and outgoing, raising levels of anxiety and confusion. As every conflict is outside of the door standing with us, it irreversibly seems the entrance to solution is an illusion.

For every program there is a struggle programmed within it to keep you in a cycle that without knowledge and wisdom, you have no exit out of. Set in stone these struggles will appear to postpone the ideas capable of opening a door closed by repetitive problems. Struggle has been implanted and persuasively designed to appear being in front of a door that can take you out of this routine is obscene. Why accept struggle?

Do you even know that you have accepted struggle?

Upon your efforts to complain, no matter the pain a struggle can develop in your life, do you understand what you have accepted by accepting the program?

Working everyday to pay a bill that will not stop in its cycle is a primitive example of struggle. Think about how they have convinced society that there is a need to survive, and now ask yourself – survive what? I assure you many readers have had a job for what feels like countless years; the same job over and over year after year.

Acceptance, who can say as of now they like exactly what it is they do because they feel comfortable doing it? Few, and that is on the account that many unconsciously work for survival of a struggle that is not designed to end. You are working a job that has proved

CC

acceptable in helping you manage struggle in your program. You are not comfortable, and you do not favor your labor as a choice occupation you find interest in. Any job can be the key to accepting struggle with complete negligence to the needs you desire to just live life. Jobs have kept you paid long enough to make payments, but also well enough to help you disregard how comfortable you can live.

You have accepted struggle and everyday you dream or visualize what living style you find comfortable, you will go back to work another day and object that vision. And now, you are leaving what opportunity possible and realizable to allow struggle to make a way of living comfortable appear somewhat impractical. We never realize what time we devote to struggle and to the conflict keeping its vice grip tight on your ideas that speak of change. The struggle compromises your ability to seek a possibility of change or fathom the idea of it.

Not only have you accepted struggle like commitment, but also you have also completely ignored the idea of entering the door closed in front of you. We question the bills backed up as well as the cars that seem to die in the usefulness to our materialistic satisfaction. Our actions in contentment with struggle are detaching our will to be brave enough to step out on the doorstep and walk through the door leaving the cycle of struggle behind. The door to exit struggle will close behind you, but by your rejection to accepting struggle, the door will never be locked.

Stress and depression can flood a town of thoughts accepting the uncomfortable position their life is currently in. Wake up and realize you are being challenged by struggle. Problems can eat at your strength leaving you with a weak mind resulting in the incognizant state to accept struggle.

Second thoughts are our minds second-guessing our actions to reveal our abilities while living through life every day and making consecutive unacceptable decisions. You have had those thoughts when you have told yourself what you wanted, envisioned the scenes of a life you wanted in your head giving you picture perfect imaginations of goals and obligations reaching a successful statues.

We let the struggle to live bully us into the reality "struggle or die." Bills have consumed your vision and you immediately get confused and backed against the door to leave struggle. You walk out into struggle and into an uncomfortable living instead of turning around and placing your back towards struggle.

God has everything here for you in the order you are destined to receive it, and as God truly believes you need it. You make up your minds attempting to concern inevitable life perplexity. In your mind, you will visualize and review difficult days at work and stressful days in life transitioning into the comfortable living of your own satisfaction. Relief is a feeling struggle can throw into your life's pool like a fishing rod. The feeling of relief makes the job you accepted working at – due to the fact it pays bills, but are living tremendously uncomfortable with – appear to be bait.

As you take the bait every day you endure this struggle, struggle pulls you out and then takes you away from the feeling of relief and tosses you back into the same pool you desperately wanted to leave. Do not let struggle take your understanding from you as your understanding of what struggle is, is important. Realization of your capability to live can aid you with advantages, which are rebellious to accepting struggle.

Barely surviving as it is, day to day choosing to rely on your acceptance, it will crumble you to an unbelievable loss of faith. This acceptance will leave you to fall under the floors of failure and break into pieces of confusion.

Reality is a fire that you can burn to an extent of death; this death is the ability to understand the activity of life. Struggle can be pain if you allow it to leave you dead to understanding. When you are dead to understanding struggle, you cannot and will not realize what your struggle is or how you have accepted it. Realization is the key to living comfortable. Your living should be as comfortable to you as it reflects your behavior and morality to those around you.

The mind will focus only on what is open to it. You can decide the opening, which can create a window of actuality leading the course of your actions in full consciousness of your abilities. Reality is a skybox, you look out and see the world moving, living, and operating as it is directed but rarely as many people individually desire freely.

In reality, problems will remain, as they exist with no change. Reality is the view of what is without alteration and the truth in it. And there is no arguing with reality because the case is closed on the nightmares and negatives. Bills, drugs, car accidents, fights, killing, rape, suicide, ignorance, attitudes, taxes and more all exist inside the original layer of reality. The actuality of your life is the control that you have. How comfortable you desire to live is in actuality yours to decide, yet, only after you have opened your mind to how you have accepted struggle. You cannot control the barriers of organized living and trying is nearly impossible without facing some form of inevitable controversy.

Realize: is to make real or actual.

Many of us have bills and bills are uncontrollable, they exist as long as money does and will. Bills are the bars to make a jail cell, the walls of separation between a comfortable realization and the acceptance of struggle. The laws of financial organization are keeping those who cannot acknowledge a door – to be placed in front of a window. Due to bills, we are brought to a mind state that buries hope, faith, and possibility into a grave. Frustration builds as it is fueled by the arrogance of struggle. Complications mentally begin sending the mind into a distrait canker. Unusual thoughts begin providing negative motives to gain an advantage over life. We allow struggle to force the weight of problems into a pound that measures up to limits, and these are limits we only have when we decide to deal with our dreams as imaginations never to become reality. We want occasionally the values of life that we deem to suit favorably in our interest.

Yet, allowing the fallaciousness of failure hack its way through what could be determination, motivation is no longer gained by self-esteem on levels higher than drugs. We fail to constantly realize the grip of negativity that keeps us in these mental illusion states, finding more reason to become angry, disorientated, and negatively fueled. Blood is replaced with stressful streams of misunderstanding pumping ignorance further throughout the body, acting off confusion and frustration instantly and unwisely.

Bills are general life issues storming upon our thoughts leaving us to lead our brains into ideas that make sense only when our objective is to survive recklessly. Shade over the negative reflection of stupidity forms the most uncompromising thoughts, and also the process of feeding stress continuously – regardless of the obvious outcome consciously or unconsciously acknowledged.

We are stuck in situations, and while cemented in, we only seem to assume ideas we have developed to overcome situations, which are either short cuts or ways to take advantage of any noun. Many of our ideas go from switching jobs for more money to deciding not to work to experience life through actions that accumulate money faster. Struggle can cause an override in the mind. This can keep us focused on what can seem like an advantage from the start of things, but at the finish line, we have spent majority of our lives focusing on what is suppose to be the short cut and advantage.

Life will be uncomfortable for years to come, and this uncomfortable feeling will persist as we continue attempting to live for a single advantage over struggle.

Our environment can cause distractions that give us extreme concerns. These concerns are growing on us and leading us into choices altering our lives negatively. Fully understanding the inconsistent thinking environmental concerns bare on our process of living, and as the events and actions of others surround us, we will process thoughts that will appear to us as options for better understanding where we stand in life. When you want to relocate from an area or change your living habits, you will give yourself options. Ask yourself what are your options? Try to understand the pros and cons of your options and individually minus the affect it may have with integrated opinions from others. We will mention – on occasion – that the answers to these questions have been thought out and reviewed previously. And, without doubt of course our intentions are to seek better, but in the transition of wanting better, where have you sought to realize the location of your determination.

Determination is a feeling so strong it can take young men surrounded by drugs, murder, and poverty and somehow transition them into the biggest motivation and inspiration for a specific talent that is now known today as "hip hop" – like Jay-Z. In other words, when you realize you do not have to accept struggle, you then enable yourself to become product spawn from great capabilities.

See whom? Me?

A mirror is more than a tool to motivate the use of adjectives. It reflects everything and holds nothing back including the bad. You look into it and you see flaws and good qualities all together. God has a different type of mirror he or she places in front of us. This mirror you cannot see your physical reflection in because this mirror rather enables you to see who you are as a person, yet, only internally.

Many are assuming they are starring exactly at who they are now when looking into the mirror God has placed before us. I indeed emphasize "now" being as though it is not who you are overtime but just who you are now. Should I investigate deeper with you? I shall. You are what you cannot see and God knows you cannot see, which is why he has placed his mirror for our use. God's mirror does not and will not reflect a face at all unless it is the face of your personality. It will not display physical features pleasant or unpleasant to the eye because none of that matters in God's eyes.

I have recorded our tendency to believe about ourselves only what we have acknowledged proof of. No word of mouth can provide just reasoning to understand a perception, opposing the current recorded perception above this sentence. Who and what we are is only brought to light in the darkness of our reflection through this particular mirror. I have seen this mirror plenty of times, as well the reflection, which is just as confusing as it is frightening.

The scariest part of being who you are designed to be, is realizing you are at the moment what you are designed not to be. Being terrified to identify who you realistically are, many of you avoid the reality – converting to creating beliefs that tell you, you are this and that, while sub-consciously knowledgeable that you are not. Principles of the imagination are being manipulated by a falsified occupancy of nouns.

Why is it we can debate right and wrong in favor of another's life at a glance, but as quickly as the glancing transition from our eyes to other to others eyes to ours, we begin the process of justifying what can be seen?

God judges all and only God judges us. The tormenting inflictions we impose on the lives of others believing what characteristics can be explained and explaining it ourselves, serves as the reason we need these mirrors in front of us. Some are still clueless as to what mirrors we are looking into, but one way I can help with that

If seeing is believing, then our own eyes will never believe the truth of who we actually are, which is the most concerning objective to us all. Reality plays little literal relevance in the deep diving analysis process we avoid. Of course what we desire to see is not illusion. In all actuality what we make real, or what we allow to persuade a façade to be real, will dominantly become our reality even if it is not. I do not make believe or encourage the strict integration of false realities in the process of thinking daily, and although my imagination runs very strong, I do intend to keep the results of my creations realistic.

God does not give you a mirror to keep you infatuated with how you personally believe you look personality wise. It is easy to create a personality we feel comfortable owning up to. Unfortunately, that personality is likely one with flaws that we can accept but also may burden us into our worst misconception of who we are designed to be. The characteristics in this personality we create are what we bargain with because we feel as though it is what best fits our life, and as well how we are living in it.

Understand that the mirror is here and it is not leaving any time soon until we see the true individual God has birthed inside of us.

Many of you have been through the awkward conversations where you have met someone new and they ask Tell me about yourself? Your response is what do you want to know? And how did you respond...

With 50% truth, 25% imagination, and 25% silence on those parts of you that really matter.

Now of course when you speak you are going to include the partial truth helping your character appear more presently comfortable to be around. Are you telling the complete truth when you answer that question, goodness no you are not. We feed so much of what we can accept and what we can believe comfortably fits into the realities of others. Yet, we ignore all everlasting factors inside the mirrors reflection. It is completely normal so do not panic. All right, the reality is it is not okay. So panic, panic a lot because much of what you are experiencing now is because you are not seeing you for what you are and allowing who you think are to co-exist with your experiences in life.

Check it out God isn't crazy or confused and neither is God lost or second-guessing any action or outcome God permits you to endure. Much of what some of us are going through is because God is not focusing on moving you onto what you desire to be. God focuses on you understanding what and who you are, and that you are that individual because God desired for you to be. It can be believed to be true in the places we want to be or a position in life we want to reach. Think about the person that you are now as far as you know, and then think about the conditions you are asking to be in and experience as that person. Assuming is bad but just assume that you are asking to be in a position your personality does not qualify you for, failure to effectively grow with endurance is a regrettable offense. You have broken into a city and began selling your falsified self to merchants who are only beneficial to you when they buy authentic resources.

It is hard to understand from me just explaining it but I promise you I am only speaking from what I have visually accepted as I have seen it. I have witnessed many of us force the belief, which is we are people holding these characteristics, which can define us, but the actual image God's mirror is displaying is showing you even more than what you thought you had inside, and even more of what you have that you do not permanently necessarily need to keep. Lies we tell ourselves we only reveal to a reality that can comprehend truth. The cycle of personalities cooperating together is constantly broken by your negligence to face the mirror and own that person you burry inside – fearful of the mask falling off in in the situations we could harvest in with our natural state of character.

I have been through a lot in my life – facing different arguments with others, sometimes very close family members and other cases socially interacting with strangers. I try to refrain from debates with strangers but it is those very moments we exchange knowledge. Those moments where we bring the unprepared identity into a situation prepared for the identity of the person you should be, are the very times where we will look back consistently at how the situation could have been different.

Alternatively back to the point, arguing to prove a point with a personality that is not your own is essentially you racing towards failure with a myth acting as your baton. Have you ever been around two friends and they are arguing heavy, and as the weight of the topic is a total misunderstanding in which you witness one person say, "you always do that though" and the other may reply saying, "you act like you don't either." That individual and the responder dwells deep into some strong point that either may not actually have interest in, at the time of argument, living up to.

Now while they both are going at it, you are witnessing two people identify what they see in the other person that he or she clearly has not seen at all or denying acknowledging as reality. It is then when we realize if it was never said they would have never discovered it. Being in the positions to sit and watch – agree or disagree – that yes these two individuals do obtain these characteristics or personality traits. Now while still on the observing end, you have to slightly intervene to help them identify the trait neither of them is willingly to recognize. Or, you may have another friend around and they will possibly say: "They both do this and that, so I do not know why they are even arguing."

This is it. This is God using another individual as God's mirror – reflecting from another mirror, which is near by – showing you the actual personal traits of a person that they cannot yet see for themselves. The mirror God places in front of you he often uses as a window for others, which can help you understand how to see yourself.

We are not always going to be able to look into our own mirror and identify the personality we obtain, and then completely accept it. Sometimes it takes some intervening with the use of others around us to observe closely. In many cases we perceive this as an individual being over analytical, looking too deep into any noun at the original layer of composition. Also, we have to identify the environmental experiences that you will go through. Certain situations you are going to go through reflect your personality off of your mirror, and thus lead you into the sight of what is really who you are.

Fighting this actuality is our built in defense system, but it is how we activate the system causing us to respond to it irrationally. Mostly this is due to us being scared of the unfamiliar. When approached with the unknown we activate our defense system from the incentives derived out of fear. Take for example the first time you jumped or leaped. Probably difficult to recollect but if you can, think about that view of how far across or how far down, the feeling that crossed your mind. Curiosity tempted you but lack of knowledge prevented you. If you jumped, it was not out of confidence and faith but curiosity. Often our curiosity can make or break us. Consequently, our fear will cause our curiosity to do nothing but break us.

I have spent my years and days and hours writing this book about how mentally challenged we are and continuously expressing situations we go through causing the challenge. From the time I begin writing this chapter, I noticed that I was going through some things in my life causing me to question myself asking, "Why am I going through this?" I challenged my self-esteem and at other times challenged my will to believe I could become capable of doing anything.

God sent me through a series of experiences that unfolded my mind, freeing it to discover what type of person I actually am.

Remember, in certain situations we go through in life we are displaying something out of our personality, and this is either emotional expression or us dealing with the situation in a certain way by action alone. Take for example a very calm person who barely gets a scare from anything. That individual could one day be in the event of a situation, one involving terror or a frightening accident that requires someone to be very patient in order to help out. Such an individual could identify his or her ability to be very patient through panicky situations, and in result develop knowledge of certain positions in life requiring patients. Are you following me?

Here let me try this – if you look back when you attended high school, or if still in school, have ever had to run from a bully or got in trouble and had to run from a teacher, and per say this is frequently. Often the witnesses of this event began telling you that you run extremely fast. You run very fast and for some, someday the running has sent you into the presence of the track team coach. Now are you following me?

That is also a true story, I know a guy who experienced that exact situation. He does not run track today, but the point is that God places you in a situation with the personality that you have, and God will require you to express certain traits from your personality that bring you to realize other traits about yourself, or certain personality traits, which can be seen as you endure life in God's designed way. Seeing yourself through God's mirror provides you the visibility to acknowledge what can be exactly the life for you. Through the situations you are going to endure you will example something in your personality that stands out, or even something in your personality that you did not know was there. The result of this can make you question who you saw yourself as before.

It is incredible the possibilities brought from seeing yourself in God's mirror. Envision multiple situations you could keep yourself from handling poorly, all due to you acknowledging whom you are. Notice back up I said that possibly you have been in the situation where you needed to explain what type of person you are, because of this some of you are cocky enough when describing yourself that may sound like this:

"This is me and most people can take it or leave it that is who I am."

And that is the most comical statement ever being as though the second you finish that sentence, you are ensuring that you know yourself completely, which evidentially you do not.

We never know ourselves completely; in fact, we are continuously going to learn about ourselves because we are in desperate need of this mirror God places in front of us. The mirror helps you see what personality you actually are displaying. Display is what you see and visually can accept is your personality in observation. I want you to begin to pay attention to what is going on through the times you experience life, when you feel as though you are in a situation that appears to be making life too uncomfortable.

Try to make something of what you go through instead of limiting your outlook to tragedy or misfortunate turnouts. A lot of the time, we go through situations and are going to do the typical, which is identifying what the situation looks like. Many of us say what if I hit the lotto or what if we came into a lot of money. What I want us to understand – together – is consider that who you think you are as a person may not be the person God wants to bless with a lot of money or provide various blessing to. That is what experience is for. It will mold you into seeing yourself as the person God intends to bless.

I know a lot of us are still starring directly in that mirror and saying everything about ourselves that we could find to fit the frame. When it comes time to seeing ourselves, we are the first to pose the question...SEE WHO? See yourself for who you are truly designed to be. Look deeper. Look into the mirror God has provided.

Compromising

CC

What I need you to understand as of now is that we all are mentally challenged. I know this is going to sound like some seven step program to get over mourning, but realistically understand that it is not.

I held my head high and what I realized is the truth many of us disregard. It always appears uplifting to think of money as a motivator, except we deactivate concerns about other topics when we do. These topics can provide better meaning into our actions revealing purpose. Such actions are debatable at a cost we do not acknowledge until our actions are reflecting a mistake.

One thing about our actions that single out our misunderstanding of our challenges is our self-dissatisfaction. You can review it in every decision after the action has been acted out. Better to be lead by comprehension than to be followed with confusion, which is the privilege of compromising with awkward reality.

I ask again, what do you want to do, and what is the purpose of wanting to do it? Do you even know or is this a question you find the answer for three seconds after you have been asked it?
I hate to bare bad news and never like telling it but most bad news is the truth, and truth is never what we like to hear. The truth is very difficult to compromise with because it various so often. The weight of the truth is a tank pushing the belts around its wheels over gravel. The leading comprehensive understanding of what one believes to be the truth is neither right nor wrong. And with that said, I ask more specifically, what do you want to do? With so many versions of the truth one could assume that many of us pick a truth we can believe in and run with it. Take for instance religion, we will all compromise with the truth of some belief and build our faith behind it as we set our goals around it. Because truth can be manipulated

there may very well be no flat out layer of the truth. Or is there?

We are depriving the value of what can be motivation for misleading concepts sourced from broken information. To elaborate, the rules of success that were, and still are today, made by people who do not have any intention on seeing you succeed. You sit before you stand and tell yourself that you need what you want. Unfortunately in most cases, what you want is not what you need, which results in you following what you believe while still unknowledgeable of how harmful it can be when you try to lead your life behind broken sources.

It is a heavy burden for my actions to bear as I am acting through reaction to understanding why I observe how some struggle. I have come to witness why others suffer and why the pain they feel is irrepressibly coming. Believe me, I want no part in telling you that you are debating your actions and your reasons with false knowledge, yet, I feel the dire need to express what God has installed inside of me for the greater benefit.

There is no cooperation within society to promote natural God Installed values. You are not acting off of a resourceful motive and receiving relative promised results. What you are doing is relying on man made instructions to guide you into what person you will become, how you will become that individual, and if you can become he or she at all. Even if the chains linking you to your misfortune were not transparent, still you will follow every link mislead and accepting the trials and tribulations sourced from the hand and thought of man. We act in response to motives, which will be for everything the results we receive are not for. Kind of like when you work hard for a blessing and finally receive it, but only to utilize it for a disadvantageous purpose – one not associated with the core meaning of your existence – and resetting your troubles.

Never easy to cope with after you take out time to reflect on the fact you did not take yourself away from a situation causing you confusion, but only to have reset the process. And yet, this is all going on up inside of your head.

I do not doubt you understand why I chose compromising as the title for this chapter, although if you do not understand I will clarify. Every single thought is processed by mind. Yet, there is a moment or more where your actions process your thoughts faster. As your actions engage, you are now dismissing the ability to process a thought, and decreasing the chances of your mind cooperating with your physical responses to the world.

Compromising is not only a set agenda between two specific terms i.e. thinking and action. No individual factor is in particular interest alone, which contradicts the previous sentence, but only to conflict with the reality that neither alone can ever produce beneficial reality, unless used together. Understand, you have wants and various reasons supporting each want you desire, yet, any reason can mislead any action resulting in you finding nothing more than less of what you could of expected, thus leading disappointment into your home of aspiration. Reason be, I have observed many of you chase money causing your actions to determine when you get it. Take a second.

I want you to see where you are not compromising, excuse me where we are not compromising.

You can have two important concerns about money. One of them is the core reason not being able to compromise is an evidential problem, which is wanting to determine when we get money.

Let me explain, you have reasons for thoughts into speech that do not compromise with your actions. One of the reasons I have witnessed is us wanting to determine when we get money because we by nature are programed to favor control. Also, as a reminder control is one of various reasons many of us are struggling. We all are trying to determine when we receive money and using control to determine the date and time exactly.

The reason does not match the action we have – to compromise with other important factors of concern – because we seek control intolerably yet with an instigated desire. That would be the how part of accessing our desires after we have activated them. How you get the money is a cyclical sought choice of various pre-developed, and yet, limited options.

I believe we need to compromise the two – reason and action – and only then will the results be what we are asking for. Here is where it is going to hit you hard, now if you have arms on the chair you are seated in, grab them. If you are sitting on the couch stand up to fall back with eyes popped like kernels.

With every compromise there is a compromising point. This can be the point where you realize what needs to be done against what can or you want to be done. This is reality because we can make a decision to act on how or when, but we only find trouble determining how. Some of us can act cooperatively on both, and if that is you then go to the next chapter this may not be for you. Seriously.
There is a point where we are confused about compromising how and when. There is a compromising point to guide us and that point is GOD.

We go through what we go through in life and are feeling like the situation is causing us to go about "when" without compromising with "how". Even if we consider the process, we do not figure the process out truly until God's presence is recognized not somewhere but everywhere. We are entitled to controlling when we

CC

get the money, but working against time you realize life is becoming uncomfortable much quicker than you can actually control if it does not. Getting to the money is not good enough and knowing it is coming is never good enough, and this is because it is written in Proverbs:

"Hell and destruction is never full; so the eyes of man are never satisfied."
- Proverbs 27:20

We want to control when and we want to control how but have lost sight of the correlating values in each. Let me give you and example.

Example

Say for instance, you are on your road to success and God is in the car with you. God informs you he is allowing you to drive. God instructs you to take the wheel and as you are steering you are deciding where you think God may want you to go. By this time, if you have not asked God where you are going, then you more than likely have attempted to anticipate your destination based upon your desires. As you are growing eager to reach the destination, you know God is riding with you and this influences you to believe he has great things for you at this destination. This is where we neglect meeting at a compromising point. First mistake, was assuming that where you want to go is exactly where God has designed you to be.

So, instantly you think to yourself and decide you are going to take the beltway because you believe it can get you where you think God wants you to be faster. At this point in process you want to control "when" you reach the destination you are headed to. By deciding to control "when", you may very well figure since you know when "how" is an anticipating obvious. The beltway is faster than your average road to success and you took the beltway because you wanted to control when you reached success Q.E.D fast.

Now here are a few mistakes with these decisions. One, you did not compromise how and when; by choosing when you figured how would follow. Two, you are missing a key point, which I will explain in just a second. Three, which is most important, you did not ask God, assuming taking the beltway would be quicker. Now back to two, when you ride on the beltway what do you see? You witness cars, dividers, signs, and locations. You also witness things at a glance barely giving you any opportunity to stop to see at all.

I know some of you have avoided riding on the beltway and what do you see on regular streets? You see people walking, cars parking, and people driving, stores, malls, gas stations, banks, and buses are all possibly visually sighted. So do you realize what you miss when you attempt to control "when" you reach what you want by the beltway route. On the beltway you do not see what you see on the regular streets. So what do you see?

You see life!

You do not see banks and people walking into stores on the beltway. You are sitting here trying to take the beltway and take control over when you experience life all while you are missing life. God wants you to experience life and that is why we need God as our compromising point to compromise how and when.

Here is your wake up call, why sometimes when you are driving you still have accidents with God in the car. At times, God allows us to drive since we do not know exactly how or when. God does this because we have to make these choices to learn from taking different routes leading us somewhere beneficial at a steady pace, or heading into disaster and

CC

disappointment at a very high-accelerated speed. God asks you to drive fully aware of the mistakes God knows we will make. Think about it, we realize when we try to decide "when" we are actually telling God no we do not accept God's guidance.

Now what we fail to realize on this ride to success is we believe cause our hands are on the wheel, foot on the accelerator, eyes on the road, and God said you could drive that you are actually driving.

God knows us and we do not recognize before we start driving that for one it is originally God's car you are riding in. For two, if you had of checked the ignition before you began driving you would of found no key in it. Had you checked the gas meter it would read empty. You really thought you were driving, and it almost felt real. I know because I have been there. I need you to understand the reason your life is still driving to success is because even when God allows us to drive, God was and is always driving. God is always moving the car along the road to success. God only wants to know if we will say yes and allow God to be our compromising point. If you will say, "God I do not know where I am going," which means that we cannot possibly control when we get there, God will reveal to you that the control is in great hands.

God is the how and the when, and when God is in control the questions are not how or when. The question is God can you be my compromising point, can you organize what I do not have in order, bring to focus what I cannot naturally give my attention to, and lead me where I am only unsure of where to go.

Compromise with what we want to understand what we need

I never imagined that I would be compromising with the reality of what world we actually live in. It is never a wake up call but more a refusal to believe that what experience and I live in is the poverty, violent, and broken societies. The road seems paved with every divider set to keep you on the side of what is and what is not. I think where people try to get me is a point where I realize what is not just is not. Realize as well that no dream is coincidence or incapably imagined. Many of our thoughts are composed from destinations installed within us. The coincidence is I am defending my standing perception, believing what is not does not necessarily mean it is what cannot be.

I want us to understand the compromising efforts we apply to our lives. I have followed the same intention since chapter two.

Listen to me when I say this because the tough things about mental challenges are that we fail to realize we can over come them. A disability is hindering thousands of individuals from mentally functioning through the use of basic behaviors. You must understand the differences from the challenges we truly possess mentally and those stemming from it. These concerns I have are challenges and grave obstacles we will endure. In the life we live today we have a choice and that is most important right now, to choose. Choose to consider to compromise so you can advance further successfully as an individual.

Believing that what is not is what cannot be and will not be is the mind of a struggling traveler on an ignorant journey. The accusations lacking faith can bring no identify. One key action that controls much of our outcome is to believe that someone telling you what is not is what will never be.

I have had people close to me and others that barely know me tell me, "That is just the way things are, there is nothing you can do about it." I hear you and I refuse to feel you, and at that understand you. It makes no sense to ever tell someone what he or she is going through mentally, over situations that exist realistically, their trials are incapable of being anything but a problem for them. I doubt you would ever understand somebody who is in a situation that makes you feel more pain than someone homeless and than someone being told that they have nothing. The worse feeling grown from being told you have nothing is to feel like it. To feel that everything you cherish and hold high is nothing but a dream behind your closed eyes at night. Why should you have to compromise with what they tell you is what it is. I know nothing is what it is because it is only what you are making it. At that what you only began to allow it to be. Do not ask me to compromise with what you are too programmed to believe is fate. I do not believe I can make an attempt to live how somebody has scheduled me to live, and who has the same organs, flesh, and bones.

Compromise with God and fend off the ways of man fighting to force you into their self-structured ideas of surviving. I care for others because I see we are not caring for what can be cared about forgotten in the cyclical process of hatred for positive progress cooperatively. We is a word that describes us all, and I feel like I have been through a pain that has robbed us all of a dream, or even a hopeful speculated inquiry on destiny. Keep your faith.

I hate nothing but dislike a lot and to accept people who feel like I belong in struggle, I refuse to. Do not allow anyone to tell you compromising is something you should have to do. They will tell you how they see it, and even with everything you have ever dreamed you do not see what they tell you to be future bound. Fragments of bad information all produce one entire whole idea of failure. Redesigning you thought process is spur from the ideas of compromise. Compromising with our own plan holds the capability of turning any bad situation into decent, but compromising with God's plan can convert any position bad into great.

Listen to me, when I say compromise I mean agreeing with certain options, mind made decisions that are going to force us into or out of uncomfortable positions in life we are programmed to endure. These decelerating circumstances planned for us are killing the prosperity value. Your plan is only of the inspiration of two sources – the misleading consequential influences of Satan or the installed values of God. Society is robbing you of every reason to believe in compromising, but the proof is in the pudding, are you going to fight to struggle or fight to find light at the end of the tunnel you didn't ask to be thrown in. Never let man or Satan burry you deeper in a hole God builds a bridge over.

It is never what we want to hear but that is the truth, and yes man will always debate this knowledge with man made reasoning, but how can we expect the truth from the mouths of men that will not let their ears hear it. I do not want to confuse you but understand you need to make a compromising effort with what is in you life's plan. Everyone is designed to feel loved, supported, and live for bigger and dire purposes.

I listened to people allow words to leave their mouth that could break every bit of hope I could have ever had growing up. I have seen the intention in a person's action to make me feel like I have nothing worth living to see happen. I have been fussed at like I was someone who never knew the definition of right. People have put my career in their negative conversations, and I know that they probably are the same ones saying I cannot make a difference. I have stood before the parents of some that I love and have informed them of what I intended to do, only to hear every word out their mouth summarize what could only be doubt. People used examples from their own life as if they were really giving you a heads up, but instead of taking my confidence for seriousness and giving me some credit to want to be big and famous. They never told me what I was supposed to hear, what I wanted to hear, what I needed to hear, what I should have heard. These people fed me their beliefs – I really knew I did not want to hear, but listened only so I could take what they said as an incentive to be something they cannot fathom possible. For belief they required proof for interest. The most difficult experience is associated with the most negative opinions coming from very negative people. It is almost as if people are trying to get you to bargain compromising with what they believe, however the point of this part of the chapter is to inform you that being what someone thinks you are going to be, or even acknowledging their suggestion, is something you can decide to compromise without.

Compromise with what you believe is and is not reality of the influenced logical ways of life. In the end, nothing will be compatible with your beliefs but the true underlying reality of life, which you receive at the compromising point. Your beliefs are your tools, perception is reality, therefore if you believe in compromising, thus compromising will transform into your reality. I do not believe many of you are going to understand this challenge until you meet it, and then find the words are not supporting but demanding you to avoid what you imply to be your current reality. Your implication – being everything you believe, is what can bring you out of your programmed situation.

I just want to you hear everything from you own point of perception. You will want to hear what you tell yourself you desire, against what you understand but also with what God tells you that you need, and then analyze to compromise to believe you can then see every perspective negativity can lead you to misunderstand.

I am not implying that you disregard what people tell you. Do not ignore advice because you are confident what you feel is right. It is more than just covering your ears and believing nothing that you hear. It is important that you understand compromising with what you hear and what you know, to come out with what God knows you need, to understand how to live life as God has planned. Do not let my contradictions mislead you into a concept that you find debatable, although I can speak on contradiction cause not everyone understands what you know the way you know it. Everyone is not going to believe what you choose to believe and the perception they receive is definitely not going to be as accurate as yours will or will not be.

In the end follow your heart to find faith in the wisdom that can lead your mind. Self-destruction begins when we fail to see through the challenges we face mentally. When we fail to acknowledge our challenges, it is then we fail to surface our strengths to overcome them.

COMPROMISE.

NOTES:

Attitudes and Judging

"It is not the behavior we misunderstand, but how to respond to it?" – Unknown

CC

I cannot help but notice how attitudes of the people become more aggressive by the day. I mean the attitudes have always been an issue but today WOW. People are using every situation or life event to determine how they are allowed to feel. At first it confused me to acknowledge how people can transition a daily attitude from a momentarily felt, or, desired one. This, as I view the tension on ones face expressing the "If only it were legal" look.

Attitudes are actually more confusing than I first thought to comprehend. Most would judge based off of facial expression. If he or she looks like they are mad then that individual must be mad, well not quite. Knowing how to read an attitude is very important and more difficult than first perceived. To read an attitude is to understand how to determine judgment. We will all judge whether consciously or sub-consciously, regards, the outcome of judgment creates the mental challenge I call Delude Comprehension.

Surely many of you have begun preaching in defense that you do not judge anyone. Why would you insist you are so un-human? People are human and humans by nature will judge. Whether you have done so intentionally or are unaware you have passed judgment fairly often.

Delude Comprehension is the cause of many poor reactions to actions, as it is also the act of improperly perceiving ones demeanor. Attitudes, personally in my opinion need, in skeptical situations, to be read. Reading attitudes reflects how you can judge a person(s) emotional state of mind. Depending on the head count, reading someone's attitude may find its purpose in judging the environment.

Now before we go any further, find no need in hiding the verbally thought obvious. Yes, in a thought once or twice you have made a judgment not even just verbally but also visually. Visually you imagine your judgment by scene into a statement or action.

Readers if I may have your cooperation, have anyone or incident brought you to anger from someone's actions towards you? Even so, I ask the same question in reference to happiness or perhaps attraction causing reaction to the action. Judgment is every little voice in your head that says what the mouth does not disclose openly, and thus is technically considered voicing ones opinion. People who upset you, perhaps a boss, and lets say a boss who has your card and is always pulling it. Say your boss continues to focus their devotion into letting you know how poorly he or she believes you do your work. As he or she informs you of what they think, what do you think?

    -Asshole
    -Annoying

Two examples are good enough, I am pretty positive your emotions take your words deeper than foul language in the event your boss chops down on your for whatever reason they find valid. Thoughts of any reaction making a label on your action, which is enforced by the individual thought, are judgments. Outspoken adjectives are projecting personal emotion in opinion, in this case, at those who pissed you off. Those individuals have given an action to gain a reaction, thus making all intentional thoughts openly expressed judgments by you to them.

Of course, people are not perfect and therefore neither can their lives be. The psychological composition unwinds as you begin to notice imperfection does not show reflection of bad, wrong, or negativity that can be explainable. Naturally, because people are people we are very observant of this fact. Judgment can post an opinion in the social atmosphere, which can produce positive acknowledgement or negative misunderstanding. Many of us will voice our judgment and cause someone to be offended (unintended) all due to us being unaware of how to read attitudes when needed. These are attitudes that will and can create the seen unseen. See what is almost obvious is to not identify what remains inconspicuous, that is sight directed towards the direction of ones emotional hidden feelings or opinion. Secluded Emotion is the concealing of an attitude that is only seen when personally provoked out. By personally, I insist the feelings supporting the attitude have been given the incentive from the source of the feelings, or recycled past feelings creating a current expression being exposed.

Deluded Comprehension brings us closer to losing control of people or situations within an environment soon to be determined harmful. Poor judgment is practically being unable to construct a thought that can connect observation and reality.

Knowing attitude can alternate responses that can create bad environments. Four people can occupy one environment, and just one of them may be having a bad day. The attitude of that individual will reflect off of that person through various forms of communication i.e. body gestures or posture – standing or sitting. Whether it is body gestures or verbal communication, the action can (more than likely will) come off aggressive or rude. Of the remaining three, another may speak to the holder of attitude and the response can and will affect the speaker. The speaker is unaware of the offense or simple wound they may have inflicted due to their lack of realization and misunderstanding. This occurs when someone feels a certain feeling and that feeling are not approached with appropriate caution through observation. As a result, the one individual with the attitude could possibly express their attitude and as a chain reaction, the person who is receiving the attitude may catch one itself.

When in the act of actually being that person having an attitude, take into consideration those around you that do not. Any certain person without an attitude is completely going to disregard the possibility of even identifying emotions shifting before it is actually an affect on the environment. Any cause can create an incident where one may feel completely isolated [Deluded Effects]. Now many of you may feel as though it is not your obligation to tend to the needs of others. While this may seem true even in literal meaning, the basic cause and effect is in case here, which nearly always results in deluding the emotions one is feeling to the environment.

The cause is when we choose to not be that eye reading what can prevent a lot of environmental disruption. We may sit sometimes and ask ourselves why one single person is feeling a little off today. The answer could be obvious but think about our lives, how often will we walk ourselves into the obvious answer? It makes more sense to be the provider of an understanding rather than a victim to the misunderstanding.

I believe with attitudes and judging the case may not necessarily be seeing that someone has an issue and feeling promptly responsible for it. The actual benefit reaches into the affects of the environment as we observe with delicate vividness. Let us consider that often times when we are experiencing or witnessing an event that looks like it is typically disturbing or strange, it is often in the environment of small or large groups of people. Think for a second about the last times you had a verbal confrontation. How many of them were where more than three people had to also occupy the environment, more than likely a lot.

Am I making a point yet?

Listen, this is what I want you to understand about the situation that you could be placed in. It will have some circumstances that will be challenging based off the environment that you are placed in. Attitudes play a huge role in the ensuring of a successful positive cooperative environment. Attitudes determine how others will reflect in the brink of any situation. It is most understandable that we can provide the possible ensuring of the successful environment with good sense of feeling. This is where judging comes in and plays its biggest role.

Please understand I am not asking you to walk into every room or building and start searching for the bad apple of the day. I am in fact saying that there are bad apples in every day, and they affect the way our situations will come about. Many of us from what I have observed are completely affected by bad attitude environments.

What is the first thing that happens when we identify someone that has a bad attitude? We at times and even unknowingly develop a bad attitude of our own. We do this based off the fact that someone has an attitude and we do not want that person and their attitude to affect us. At this point, an instinctual defense mechanism activates and creates a defensive deflecting feeling. View it as a defense mechanism preparing for the worst before the better.

I once walked into my job and the manager had an attitude. One of my co-workers will help me acknowledge this by informing me before I even identify their demeanor (Kendra). Knowing this, I prep myself for the possibility I may have to involve myself in a verbal conversation with the manager. Now just as I heard and adjusted my attitude – knowing I have to interact with this piss poor attitude manager, I also witnessed other co-workers identifying just as I have the bad demeanor, entering the same preparation as me except they found more incentive to gain an attitude just as bad as the manager. I believe many of us call this the "Wish someone would attitude."

It is the creative nature of being human with tendencies to react before understanding action. Fairly the point to make is you can be corrupted by the attitudes of others and this corruption can affect the environment that you are in by fashioning up a wave a bad energy.

The effects of a negative environment are going to come very close to making you feel as if you are finding stress in the places you routinely have to visit. Stress is stress, and let's faces it no one wants stress? Right. So the whole purpose of attitudes and judging is to give you the knowledge to identify – in yourself – what qualities are quite fond to bringing upon a negative environment, which can affect you unfavorably. Poorly energized environments – causing many of us to crack open and let stress all inside – are becoming the water breaching the haul constructed around our characteristics, thus making us characters of depression. How this happens, many of us take what we influenced on routine, not just verbally but behavior driven, and rebuild our methods of talking, acting, and thinking to fit the fond bond stitched between who we are and what we are around. Challenges are first confronted by the thought, yet, when we choose to ignore the thought, or perhaps the opportunity of thinking, and then made out by the physical.

Thought of the day: If knowledge is valued and contains certain information that provides you with the ability to become a well developing dealer of situations, why would you avoid it?

Every day we enter situations and find every reason to interact in the situation and leave with either half ass or no results, or both. In order to learn your environment, it is best wise to learn that which occupies it most, people with attitudes. Having an attitude does not necessarily mean you feel negative.

Yet, while stereotyped into typicality, having an attitude simply means you feel some particular way.

Here is where we make the rarely identified connection between the real mental challenges we suffer, and the titles we place on individuals who have to live with a particular disability limiting them from functioning by thought control. Many of the individuals are likely still trying to read and write, and this is over the age of twenty-one. Others lack the ability to observe any multiple targets at once to analyze and conclude the fruition of a situation – harmful or avoidable. To protect that from happening if we just think and consider the cause and affects of attitudes we can possibly help ourselves walk into more welcoming environments even at the realization of a present attitude.

Think about it...

Download

Mind over matter, and that means I put my mind over what matters to consider what actually does. With our eyes blood shot of grief and ears torn of stress, we are waking up to a reality battling with how to commence the work of our dreams. I feel the need to birth a solution to this bewilderment would only be a pollution to our problems. No man neither woman obtains the mind to construct a solution to our well-needed change. Yet, a force of energy and being of power well-misunderstood holds the true solution(s) we seek.

Our brains are becoming the leading cause of our self-inflicted destruction socially. The use of the brain is becoming scarcer to change, and as we live each day, I see us enforcing the rarity more than ever before. No one is thinking. No one is processing thoughts collectively and respectively to make the right decisions. Distancing our thoughts has created this disconnecting lane, and this lane takes us from the area in our minds where we can begin the development of a pattern that can coordinate a train of thought.

"We need to grow to lead ourselves as individuals before we ever consider leading each other." – Cori Coleman

We have a mental desktop and it is necessary that we download our information onto it. Store it. Keep it for as long as you like but as long as you have the information-stored period. Does this give you any urge to review the chapter titled "Location?" Viewing useful information as it is displayed but forgetting to store it is like seeing a sign that is instructing you to take a left and instead you only recall that the letters on the sign were white.

Life is evolving around us and people are picking up different taste, habits, and attitudes, and this process will continue, and as it does with the way we cope with the process of change we should be more beneficially consuming. Courageously we must go up against the turning tables and opening and closing doors creating the recycled process of deception.

Be mindful of the facts we ignore as this evolution within our societies embraces the ideas of leaving many blind to obvious inconsistencies, pertaining to financial and social factors. Information shared between the two either remain hidden if beneficial, or are strategically broken into partials and organized into levels of distribution – one can either keep up with unsuccessfully or use improperly. The partials of information are increasing and we are allowing that information to become subjects for disclosure at the bay of others will and not our own.

So heavily infatuated with the present and the future, the knowledge we leave behind is the reason the knowledge ahead of us is so difficult to deal with. As of today information is being hidden from us, by us.

Tell me how are we actually using our brains today?

The sight of growing ignorance within our societies is beginning to become overwhelming. Leading the blind into a floorless room, surely the odds of walking are narrowed down to barely one step.

"A bird sitting on a tree is never afraid of the branch breaking, because of her trust is not on the branch but on its own wings. Always believe." – Chris Sopa

Without secluding yourself to one particular process of receipting information, you can and are being advised to educate yourself to the point you can trust in your own information. As a group of humans all under the title human, the cooperation of our living patterns are exchanged selfishly. Even if information has to be individually installed, once absorbed it can be cooperatively and considerately distributed. While many of us actually do find it interesting to learn, for others it takes the eyes of the mind and an interest as direct as a needle entering a vein.

Even today all ages and cultures bare the similarity of misusing knowledge.
Knowledge is not always in the classroom so using the excuse of foreigners having the accessibility to free tuition and school is far past over exaggerated. Information is everywhere and can be downloaded at any point and time of day. The ideas of one individual and the opinions of others are all sources and types of information, yet compiled beneath the controlled distributed knowledge of the program makers.

As teens growing into adults the responsibility to acknowledge the information is really up to you. Becoming seekers is one sure way to access information withheld from you. As adults, the acknowledgement of particular valuable information should be a routine like making payments on a monthly bill. It is completely up to you to determine the cause and what exactly you are learning behind it. Easily is the mind confronted and intimidated by a group of words with a meaning, but the determination of a seeker encourages arrogance necessary to teach information one has acquired.

Imagine the possible concepts we can evaluate with the perception of several who are intend to learn and then teach all from natural interest.

Growing up is the process I feel we most may confuse with the over exerted terms mature and immature. Something's in life just are not about maturity first. First you must avoid being misled by a traditional cycle of information they have been teaching over and over for years, which will dwindle your pure interest to self-sufficiently learn. In a country where freedom is sworn into our availability, why does it seem that everything obtainable is privileged? Controlled learning.

Driving has become a privilege, they tell you specifically you are not free to drive you are privileged. Yes the order must be maintained by at what cost, we are only limited to the disclosure of information when others see fit for us to acquire it. I know middle school students who drive beyond better than most adults.

Is anyone else clueless to the freedom seen in that statement?

Growing into the society, early age or not, understand that what you know can profit your existence and how you exist. Today's living is so programmed and ruled over it isn't even hidden anymore, unless you are ignorant by choice. And unfortunately that is the mental challenge, suffering from the willing efforts to remain ignorance by our own option. The limitations are building by the rates of success from those who are actually trying to change how we can succeed. We are growing into information that gets downloaded as rules developed by man. God is almighty and above, who is Man but flesh of his image?

The authority of those born into higher power and their predecessors have been abused, as a nation, we are ruled over by information that is instructed to be embedded instead of optionally appointed and sought over. Who controls what goes in the library? Why do you have to go to school to be a lawyer instead of walk into any library and research the rules and regulations of such art of debate for just cause?

Or, take dress code for example, this information has been downloaded for years under the opinions of a set group of people who formed in agreeable cooperation, and determined suits were formal. Consider what has been learned, information has been shuffled around only to manipulate those who can be controlled.

Yes, I understand that things are as they are now, but change is in the individual first before the society. That is in fact how we can change together by changing ourselves as individuals. We grow into the stories of what should be and what is supposed to be when instead we should be growing into creating our own stories defining our own destiny.

I honor the lord, no man on this earth regardless of salary, title, or position will disable my capabilities of becoming successful.

Learning is the objective and what you are learning is imperative to your understanding before you download it. The ideas of mankind destroy our free mind and our once open – now closed – attentiveness to limitless exposure to beneficial information. Challenged by information, battled by decision to translate, we find great difficulty organizing our thoughts to utilize outside information. This is just my personal opinion, but I see no sense in the use of laws if we speak of freedom so confidently. Downloading reality is actually the true idea of progress.

Have you ever dreamed or imagined you were:

- Rapping
- Acting
- Doctor
- Marine
- Singer
- Dancer
- Comedian

Take all of the above and imagine them as pictures. And just as you envision these soon to be realities, someone comes and says, "Keep dreaming" or "Back to reality." Imaginations are not to be lived in they are to be lived out. If you can think it 9 times out of 10 you did it or said it, can do it or can say it.

Every time you are imagining your success and someone attempts or breaks that focus, it seems as if things never were imagined, that is not reality. Reality is only were your dreams vividly imagined exist. Keep imagining you goals coming true because it is healthy for the mind and your challenges of understanding life. Imagining allows you to mentally confirm the manifestation of everything you desire to do for your life.

I ask, how is living comfortable a dream? Even so, how is it not reality?

What you dream of doing in life is reality, as you live and chase it to the fullest you are living it out.

I used to believe myself that the reason we will not succeed is because of reality. The truth is that the causes of our failure are the fact we believe reality is something that does not contain our dreams. I used to stare at the T.V. screen and look amazed as I downloaded all sorts of dreams and wants. I never once saw the idea in seeking those dreams and wants through my actions because I feared my reality was to concrete.

This is the connection; information is always going to inform us of the where a bout's to find a successful chase. The crime we commit to our mind is when we ignore the information that interests us, and in doing, we further more cannot achieve along the paths of life.

Downloading is a process of taking everything you learn and using it as the keys to unlock the doors to your progression. Many of us have avoided downloading

CC

information so often we fail to even acknowledge the idea or word, progress. Using the mind as frequently as possible can alter the definite down falls promised to us, by living in these programs that keep us mentally challenged. We are indeed mentally challenged in this matter. Look at all we go through, all the obstacles in life and all the trails we as individuals face. With that said I find the need to encourage the second most concern with living mentally challenged.

Download

We need to accept the information around us, and before us, and use it to create ourselves in the image best found suitable in the world around us.

The lives of others depend on the information you know whether you believe it or not. Every day you will socialize with others and they will bring up topics, which keep you interacting into their communicable circles. Simple words used to create subjects and explanations contain parts of information that are incredibly useful amongst our living patterns. If you do not know what I am talking about I am referring to opinions.

Opinions are one of the most influential learning centers in the history of communication and education. Yes, learning center is the exact description because within opinions lies the merger between what is true by logic and what is true because of the power in belief supported by information that has been installed. Within both areas are bits of information that support either all truths or all lies. Either area can be investigated and information derived from the core of your opinion. An opinion is simply composed of what you think you know, what you have learned, and what you determine is real from both.

Everybody has an opinion and everyone uses theirs in the act of determining right or wrong, even the situations that require a task that determines your reflection as a person. That type of opinion is called "best judgment." The best judgment we use in order to determine what our opinion is and how to use it.

Look at what years of opinions have brought us to. Look at the age of technology we are involved in due to the brink of opinion. If you remember a little back in my passage, I mentioned that the dress code was of issue to the download of misleading knowledge, which we take in. Dress codes, foods, and cultures as well as all the other interesting stuff that I have become too lazy to name are all developed through opinion. Once again, a group of people agreeing on the same idea is what has made up society today.

What is an idea?

You do not need a rocket scientist to answer this one. An idea is an opinion, a self developed method of solution, plot, or planning to affect some sort of outcome or change. We have battled with opinions for years and some opinions have brought us the dangerous society we live in. Other opinions have created the speedy evolution process we have entered today.

History is full of opinions, which have determined many of our living styles. Now as I do bring this to your attention I am not suggesting you disregard the traditions of history. I will be completely honest, I am a growing human being as anyone else, and I have the full right to live how I want as it is abiding under the lords will. In other words, this is the challenge my friends. We are not taking what old method of evolution and amelioration to become better than what struggle has been programmed upon us. This is to all nationalities, I dare a single orientation read my book and suggest this issue is surely black concerned. This failure to download is bigger than race or culture. Wake up because no one is getting the easy hand anymore we all are struggling and becoming the bottom shelf item.

CC

I want you to listen to what I have written for you
and ask yourself as you finish reading — what question
will I need to ask myself to approach my opinion and
analyze it carefully enough to download the information
necessary to efficiently improve my situation in life.
Take a look at what you like, dislike, honor, and disobey.
The key to success in your life rest directly in the core
of your opinion, all you have to do is bring it out.
Download the information, as it is key to understanding
that which you are destined to become. Understanding
you is the most profitable outcome in the process of
living and breathing. We may continue to be
misunderstood but you can allow yourself to
understand how you affect others through your
decisions, actions, and reactions. Knowing yourself
allows you to take others opinions and build your
knowledge from their shared voices.

We are all looking for that top dollar, and also that
well developed scheme to plot on the wallets and bank
accounts of other citizens in America or the world.
Think about what there is to know about life and the
information you can take in from what is put out by
everyone. How about you start where it counts by
listening to information provided by each other and
download it. We are all looking for change but limiting
ourselves as we find contentment in what we only
discover by fate.
Life is more than what the challenges of the mind
limit you to. Our brain is the substance of who we are.
The power to believe can be utilized as we confront all
formats of information and carefully analyze how to
convert what is taught, researched, and exchanged
verbally into pieces of valued wisdom. Wisdom is a
download worth every megabyte.

Begin the Download now.

Truth is

"Perception is not always reality." – Wayne Chang, Pikasso Kutz

Truth is...

Truth is what we never want to hear. The truth is everything we want hidden from us as we persuade ourselves daily we deserve to hear it. A lie can make a change better than truth can make a difference. Why? People are attached to lies. We are infected with the knowledge of memory and mistake, the recollection of trail and error and have feared the results of either gravely.

Truth is some form of information you do not want to acknowledge, or, something you cannot believe you just heard, or something someone told you, which nearly seventy percent the time bares urgent news, which also is never positive. We lie because lies keep our minds and hearts in a better place, or what we perceive to be an eternal comfort zone. Those who are lied to will be more convinced to understand and forgive when lied to because they fathom the flexibility of a tattletale. Liars are most reluctant to undergo forgiveness.

Truth bares the horror and unfortunate liability of releasing the mind to freedom from thinking, and thus the promotion of untamed reactions. These reactions are so deep they can hardly ever receive forgiveness. Here is the sad part about truth. The shy reality we all hide behind – only cause we can and it feels comfortable, is truth is a makeup of lies with explanations. Obvious right? No, hence the fact we hide behind the reality of it. Truth is lies composed of misleading topics with reasons of why the misleading has occurred.

We are not honest of our kind; neither can we forgive enough to allow what can be called a lie to be forgiven even as truth is accepted. We feed lies with our own misunderstanding of what we cannot and do not understand but attempt illogically.

Example, if you suggest or reference advise or describe, you are not telling what is factual. You are not implying truth in word resourced by first origin of knowledge. You are assuming as much as suggesting, guessing with the sponge you call your brain, which instead of draining the bullshit you have soaked up for years, you wash your life's windows with this sponge full of misunderstandings.

We are not honest and mindful because honesty has no suggestions, no advice, and no describing. Honesty has definition and the definition itself displayed intrepidly. Ever question yourself using the questions "I think this is.... or I am not sure but I believe that is," if so then these particular questions are not truth.

The information is not of permissible knowledgeable exchange from one mind to another. If you have to think, wonder, or bargain from last optional thought or knowledge then it is not truth. I will not beg for you to understand the truth of my learned facts, I dare not ask or your comprehension in such a way.

Understanding the truth is of great use when tragedy can be a tool for negativity. Honesty is honesty when integrity inspires a shameless driven act. This is sad but this is reality and it will not change yet. The world has chains and we are shackled at our brains.

You are ...not true.

Let us be honest with each other, allow me with the most appreciation for your ears to be most comfortable with informing you how I have trained my thoughts. My mind is a two-lane road, a street with open exits that are all asking me to take and make that so interesting turn down a path that holds a different definition of open opportunity. Truth is but two realities. One form is the logical A to B and so on connection. The second form is the manifestation of your understanding of logical reality, combined with the innovation of your talented mind. Both enable visual and physical real. Using these forms, I have created a process of analytical behaviors, which I step by step pursue in order to seek out the truth in every given presentation of ambition. By envisioning these expectations – theoretical at beginning – I can further merge two realities to distinguish parts of truth. Opportunity is revealing its doors through this process.

How would you define opportunity as a way out an outlet from such terms as confusion or frustration?

I am observing others witness the brighter side of life through the misfortune of others. The complaining of others as well as the success of others is rather coincidently uplifting. Quite the mislead, but it is this pair of our complex virtues keeping man occupied with fighting for power. We do not need power and here is our chance to bring such a realization to the forefront. The rising climate on the issues of poverty can help challenge the weak minded to be strong and the strong minded to move out with purpose.

Where is the exit to the uncomfortable means of tolerance, which we undergo in effort to believe there are routes made to free us. How do you allow the passion to provide yet become a difference amongst those of great doubt and benefit, overseeing the less fortunate with a laugh in the face, giving the 101 pep talk on how to get better? Bullshit can stare you in the eyes many times before you believe that it is bullshit staring you in the eyes. It can make the soothing remarks to your ear, gaining not only attention but also acceptance of your approval inviting bullshit into the reality you envision.

Possibly, I find my attitude seeks the calming of character in those who have been enraged by the misunderstandings of their adversities. I have elected my patience to find truce between my emotions and how they interfere with the possibility of me finding clarity within my closing issues. To know what I did wrong, I must not allow my feelings to interfere too strongly with how I can see the original layer of reality. I personally hold the stand offish "Fuck off" high above my head leaving the "Go to hell" demeanor around my smile. And this is a reaction to actions performed by others towards me. Complications arise when I allow myself to react (as many of you have) and hinder myself from seeing through a situation to discover how I could have, or can change the circumstances – whether current or past due.

People are so uncompromising and because of those only willing souls, when they are granted the sight of advantage, will permit others to cooperatively coexist with them. What can actually be the challenge when the core decision is to help? Unrealistic facts stand and state as there are more of us bearing the attitude of help me so I can get over on you and help myself; a dirty exchange in most need of unbearable cleaning is the act itself, using one person as a stepping stool but making him feel like an elevator with greater purpose. If you are wondering how does this play in together, well it is evident that in the midst of our reaction to others we are likely to become just as they are, and thus the product of negativity we once saw reason to defend against. For example, when someone curses or gets smart with you, you would then respond with_____.

Sure.

We all know our first line of defense is to dish back what we are taking in. Yet, it is that very behavior keeping us from seeing all the key points in any situation. To see the underlying original layer of truth it will take some over-analytical tolerant endurance. Every situation has an original layer of truth, revealing the purpose and cause and effect of the circumstances created, or as some would like to describe – fate developed. Truth is but the first layer of reality, a layer

CC

built upon many years ago and tucked beneath several layers of misleading information portrayed as truth in the rarest of forms.

We do not want truth to walk along our tongues while we are fearful of the information that it holds entrapping us. But ask yourself this, if you are witness to the original truth, is it not calming to be buried beneath it as opposed to being submerged beneath lies?

Lies are decoded through the reality of actions, the mere image of the dysfunctional brain. Bravery is an act even in verbal expressions, but just as well it takes bravery to display honesty. Unfolding the truth only as it is, is effective in the ways we find it beneficial to us, as it decomposes ones individual strength in the situation when delivered to others. Which is actually a lie. Any truth unfolded before the primary or the secondary is beneficial nonetheless. Everyone needs the truth. Like I said, everyone needs the truth, this is not me clarifying everyone can handle it.

Mental retardation is a condition life lasting and on going. Those suffering and enduring their gifts have committed suicide, been mistreated by their house councilors or guardians, poisoned, treated unequally on levels of inhumane behavior even undisclosed in this book, and also the biggest form of tragedy, being simply ignored until death. This is truth, harsh and real yet fairly unbearable to some. These gifts are not challenges. Failing to speak proficiently enough to relay the misconduct acted upon you is not a challenge. One does not take classes to learn to keep from being harmed for being legally blind, mute, or deaf. The challenge is in the aggressors who take strike on these beautiful people. The truth is that the challenges are ours to bear.

Every day it is up to us to make conscious and considerate decisions that benefit not everyone but every piece to living out this puzzle we call life. Eventually, some day we can put all the pieces together and see the bigger picture. Love is such a flaw in the eyes of man, but by God's word and Jesus the Christ testimony, love is the gravity, the atmosphere, the core of the earth, and the oxygen of the planet. Challenges begin from the mind and down, but it only appears to be perceived in such a way. Truly our challenges never leave our mind. Every situation we endure in life is a mental challenge. Yet, we have the power to overcome how we conduct our thoughts and manipulate the false realities to see the real one, just to endure life through living it and not surviving it.

God did not create competition, man did. And it is man who continues to spin the web entrapping trillions of people in cycle's earth can only sustain a limited amount of life. This earth is designed to sustain continuous life, yet man has modified it so, today it only appears to behave to comfort a particular form of traditional survival. Lies of man are the persuasions of demons.

Original Truth:

The break of words or pause of inference causing the slight noticeable difference, expresses how our words are sitting in a lake only connected to an ocean forming a body of lies.

The evidence openly stands out that we are constantly giving out information that has been altered. Many of you are aware of the partial truth. The side of the story that sounds less likely to be in the speaker's negative projection. Providing information explaining all of what we want to appear convenient is partial truth. Or, in other words truth we are comfortable with.

People will tell you everything about themselves, their own life, people involved in their life, but never give you the full description of what they really think.

You know, the part of life where they hinder themselves from cooperatively interacting with every form of information they can and will provide. The words will sound smooth in a way, and as you listen may feel you are getting absolute honesty. However, the message sounds so broken into pattern. Some of what we say sounds too dull to give a sense of actuality while other parts of our speech may be interesting or humorous. Contagious are the words of a liar, seeking all who disbelieve while giving those who already do an extended misunderstanding.

Why do we remain so challenged by the decision of honest communication?

We are allowing the broad fear of consequences for our action scare us into saying everything that can be misunderstood, but sounds soothing to the ears.

The open lane of verbal cruelty, is this not how we communicate?

Liars get a kick out of lying when they can accomplish it so easily, and being believed – because the truth about truth is we actually do not want to hear it. Sure many of you say this and many will say they know this, but I ask only in interest, what is the purpose of a man knowing fires burns, if he still intends to attempt to burn it with water? Many of you will breech the question of popularity when the truth has reigned obvious "What did you lie for?" is that not obviously identifiable?

People who lie know what misdirection people have when it comes to truth. Never can you hear what was explained and be entertained by the fact, which is also involved with being honest. Yet, you choose to find more anger in the idea of one lying. Simple minds develop simple actions and those actions will never know an extravagant life. It goes for reactions simple minds develop simple reactions.

If one is to remain blind, not an individual who suffers from visual blindness, but an individual who can see through his eyes but not through his mind. Perception is reality and such a thing is either accepted or created. Mentally we fall short of the idea to accept what can be not noticed but through mental amelioration identified as positive. Our minds must undergo thought revision and advancement to organize how to conduct our thoughts at will. This process enables the mind to resurrect the lost concern and bring light to its existence, in order to find truth beneath layers of lies. We as people are so challenged to the truth that we fail to uphold the opportunity to see truth from a pure format.

Note:

Peace before truth:

We fuse genders to try to establish some grounds of contrasting excuses to use against one another in effort to seek some advantage over the other. Are we forgetting the overall truth of our existence? We all are human and make the same mistakes point blank period. While not exact in time or occurrence still the fault is universally constant, mistakes are inevitable. Women and Men bicker amongst each other over mistakes, which have caused more distraction to living life, which unruly is the actual goal of our purpose.

Instead, causing breakouts of frustration between who is right and who is wrong leading through lies and honesty, we find that the differences in gender are merely manipulated into a complication. This challenge has to be so important yet simple, getting over it only requires common sense, which with us today isn't so damn common. Before any situation can come to rise, you as a person need to understand what the truth is when you are asking for it to come before you.

Truth is a realization of what is actually going on around you but you do not notice it as society has painted over the same picture consistently. Process in your mind that the information you may be looking for, or either just being informed of, will be negative.

Now back to the idea of coming to an acceptable stage of being informed. We are going to overreact over the truth when we can already prepare our minds for what basically will end up obvious. I'll use the most common example ever.

A couple finds out that a partner inside the relationship is cheating. You know but have not yet confronted the situation with your information, yet you still wait on their information. Once you know what is wrong, at that moment I can agree with a little acting out of character it is sudden of the moment and you do not see it coming. But, if you already are aware of the problem then be realistic, it is no point on developing emotions after you have already identified what is wrong and later are now confronting it. You are building an emotional battlefield that you are walking onto just to fight by yourself. The fighting takes place when you decide you want to holler and scream and curse over an issue you are bringing to the table, but was aware of far before you did so. Any other action you may choose to display is the fighting as well when you do not organize your feelings beforehand.

Now after all of that, the person who lied or was wrong in general, they are not on that battlefield with you. Yes, I am sorry to inform but you are out there on your own. When someone who has lied or is wrong and is still at bay to lie but are confronting the situation, they are not looking to act out and express emotions they only want to get to the solution. Think about it, that's another point also, off topic, whenever you are in the wrong, truly you are not trying to stay in the wrong because you want solution giving you an outlet from judgment. So what do you think the wrong doer or liar wants? We know what can come of truth and we still choose to dual out our emotions with ourselves. Next, the partner confronting the situation is making the deal bigger than what it can be over truth you were already aware of.

You are giving a very poor effort to bring peace and an even weaker effort to create peace in an uncontrolled situation.

That is why it is easy to tell a lie and as well accept lies far greater than you can ask for truth. You will ask for the truth but after you hear it and deal with it ask yourself was all of that worth it. You honestly probably would rather to hear a lie. We play games like we really want the truth and truthfully we do not. Stop lying to yourself about the truth, God makes the truth obvious to us. All he wants to see is how we are going to deal with it.

Truth is not what we want to accept neither bargain with. We use truth like a jump rope going up and down with our emotions for the fun of it, while a rope of reality in solution goes around us. If you have ever jumped roped before think how often while doing it you are visually paying attention to the rope? You are not, you see it as it goes around you but your focus is devoted to jumping up and down.
The truth is around us all the time and we ignore it until it feels as if we are directly affected by it. How are we being so mislead by the challenges of our mind?

We do not think.

We do not consider information to keep us aware of the reality of what truth is and the effects truth can actually have on us. When the situation comes for it we all will lie. All of us will sit there and say everything we do not even believe ourselves simply to gain advantage or outlet from a situation. Now, I am not saying we repeatedly perform this act, but the odds are high if we are talking about occurrence. While talking with your family and friends you speak as if your understanding of communication is that fluent in providence of right and wrong. It is not and we all play with the truth by presenting such a misleading myth.

Our challenge mentally is the fact we cannot accept the reasoning skills to understand how to deal with truth and lies. It is an individual solution and nothing I can further tell or advise. That is not my purpose to give you answers because God has answers. I do not have the answers myself but God speaks through me and delivers some well-needed information that can lead to solutions.

We will continuously argue with these challenges and the confusion will build but as you do become more convinced that you do want a difference. Use yourself, as the first tool to develop your questions then bring them to the only energy that knows the answer. Living with the truth is hard, but understanding a lie is debatable.

My point of this book is to help you realize, we service individuals with mental disorders who do not have challenges. Currently, we live in a society under a government we do not need. But who can change that? We can. Our challenges begin in the mind and the quicker we change how we think, the faster we can change the society around us. Change you and change together, and then change the society, further more change the government. We pay for resources that are technically free. We give authority over ground no man owns. We market our lives to media just for a chance at survival. Life is not to be survived and the nations under control are forced to believe they must compete to live. Everything on the earth has proven to coexist in a cycle where life continues except humanity. Fight the program, live for each other and not against each other as we are being trained to do. Money is a crime all in itself. The use of it is an abomination. We fight with other countries over greed. There are enough resources to go around and the changes necessary to make this evident first start with you. Inside your mind are all the keys to life, yet man have made doors they have convinced you none of those keys can unlock. This is a lie.

On each side we will fight our self mentally because of the confusion we self establish rejecting what can be obvious to us. Stop misunderstanding the truth about yourself, stop misunderstanding the truth about others, and stop misunderstanding the truth about life.

We are Mentally Challenged.

Closing remarks

This book is dedicated to my son Cori "dink dink" and my mother Deirdre.

Here, I find that at the end of this journey you will not look at life for what life is making you but actually accept the reality of what you are making yourself. Together we can accomplish much more than the individual efforts we enforce around each other. I dare you to be a better person I dare you.

Ladies be women and take care of yourselves. God has given you so much love and I beg you to use it with the heart and mind both synchronized to your morals. The devil first enticed Eve, a woman, because she bears so much love it can over power any force of hatred. Today, Satan aims no different.

Gentlemen we must be very thoughtful of each other. We show each other more hatred than the people who actually hate us as a group. I am not fearful of my brothers neither will I be feared by my brothers nor will I engage into the ways of the enemy against my brother. Unity is our key as we have strength and strategy installed within us. Use it to bring life and sustain it, not over power it and control it.

I want to send a special thanks to my brothers, the oldest brother Keith Mitchell. You took me in and basically gave me a path of guidance and responsibility; I am forever grateful and love you. Tavain Hargrove, thank you for all your support and words of encouragement, truly God blessed you with the gift to heal with enlightenment, and I love you. Lamont Strong, you know you been with me riding this book out and sincerely thanks a lot for your support and your older brother knowledge (even though we are practically like the same age), you are fierce and know well of wisdom, use it. Ray, I know we had some hard times, but I still love you because your drive is unstoppable and our unity is not impossible. Jamie, man I don't think I would of ever smiled in the house without a conversation from you, you are a true inspirer and I implore you to continue to learn as knowledge is your tool. Todd, I would never forget about you, I love you be safe. I love you all. Devin, Maurice, Kevin, Debbie, Nana, and others I could never forget the support and wisdom you all have shown me over the years, thank you and I love you all.

This is an extended special thanks to my brother and friend. Bruce, a leader who has grown throughout life whisking intelligence around his image like a wizard and wand. You have been just as devoted as I to the completion of this book. When times became harder than hard, you set aside your own time and responsibilities to assist me in unfortunate times. Thank you so much.

A special thanks and recommended reference to Ceazzar Corleone, a writer, poet, spiritual leader, and more importantly a body of wisdom awaiting the recognition to expose his education.

Auriel, your life has been just as rocky as mine. Nonetheless, it is no mistake that blessings create better people and it is evident the single blessing we have received is transforming us into greater people. Never give up. I love you.

Last but not least, Greg I love you my brother. We have been in it since middle school and nothings changed. I obviously see you were my older brother, my cousin, my homeboy, and to be honest the first real friend I ever had. You are a true family man, an excellent example of a go-getter, and absolutely incontrovertibly one of the greatest kindest human beings I have ever met. Thank you.

I appreciate any and everyone who has supported me through this journey, and to that I say thank you all.

Stay together stay focused.

"The power of love is greater than any adversity. Love is the energy powerful enough to rebuild lives and societies. Love is a gift and a gift to be sent out universally."

- Cori Coleman

CC

www.ingramcontent.com/pod-product-compliance
Lightning Source LLC
Chambersburg PA
CBHW030310290526
45785CB00001B/284